Classrooms observed

To Lee

Classrooms observed

The teacher's perception and the pupil's performance

Roy Nash

Routledge & Kegan Paul
London and Boston

233856

First published in 1973
by Routledge & Kegan Paul Ltd
Broadway House, 68–74 Carter Lane,
London EC4V 5EL and
9 Park Street,
Boston, Mass. 02108, U.S.A.
Printed in Great Britain by
Butler & Tanner Ltd, Frome and London

ISBN 0 7100 7679 7 (C)
0 7100 7694 0 (P)
Library of Congress Catalog Card No. 73-82369

Contents

Tables

Figures

Acknowledgments

This work is substantially based on research carried out for the degree of Ph.D. at the University of Edinburgh during the years 1969 to 1972. I am grateful to the Social Science Research Council who supported me with a grant throughout this period. Professor Liam Hudson and Dr Albert Pilliner, my supervisors at the Centre for Research in the Educational Sciences, are due my formal thanks for all the advice and encouragement I had from them. I must thank also the advisers, teachers and children who were generous enough to co-operate with my research. They cannot be named here but I remember them with gratitude. I would like to think that they approved of what I have made of my experiences in their classrooms. Since this book is sometimes implicitly critical of teachers it seems only just to mention those among my own teachers, Mr and Mrs L. Richardson, Mrs M. Batstone and Dr J. Klein, who, at various times, have gone out of their way to help me. Finally, I must acknowledge that material in chapters 3 and 10 has appeared in *Educational Research* and the *British Journal of Sociology* respectively. Chapters 2 and 4 are based on articles written for *New Society*, and I thank the editor for his permission to include them here.

Chapter 1 Introduction

No researcher starts his work with a blank and open mind. My approach to the study of learning in schools has been influenced by two important experiences, first my undergraduate studies in the social psychology of education and second, my experiences as a schoolteacher.

At university I was taught the traditional empiricist methodology of British social science: the procedures known to economists as the input–output model. In educational research this has usually meant measuring a number of input variables, for example, IQ or social class, of a sample being subjected to different educational environments, for example, streamed, non-streamed, selective or comprehensive schools, and measuring the changes in the output variables. Let us suppose that we want to know whether anxious children learn better in structured or unstructured classes. Following this model we would take a sample of children defined as anxious and after half had spent a year or so in structured classes and the other half a comparable length of time in unstructured classes we would administer a number of standard tests and see what differences the two treatments had made. The great weakness of this model is that though we might be able to conclude (if that was the way the results went) that anxious children learn better in structured classes, we would have little idea why. In order to discover that we would have to pay some attention to the different contexts of learning provided by structured and unstructured teaching methods.

Studies of this sort have revealed a number of determining factors almost all of which have been closely correlated with social class membership. The gross facts presented by, among others, Gurney-Dixon (CACE Report, 1954), Crowther (CACE Report, 1959) and Floud, Halsey and Martin (1957), are obvious enough – the lower a child's parents' social class the poorer the child's attainments and the earlier his age of leaving school are likely to be. Unfortunately, because it totally ignores learning processes within the school, this research cannot explain the causal relationship reflected by the correlations. Early educational research tended to focus not on the school, where education is supposed to take place, but on the home. Fraser's (1959) study identified the most important factor determining a child's progress at school as 'parental encouragement'. Douglas (1964), Wiseman (1964), Mays (1965) and Douglas, Ross and Simpson (1968), all following in the methodological footsteps of this earlier work, also investigated the relationship between the home and the school and found similar results. Klein's (1965) more sophisticated sociological analysis suggested that the causal relationships between socio-economic variables and attainment might be due to subcultural differences in children's levels of aspiration and in their ability to postpone gratification. These dispositions, it was argued, may have their origin in the distinctive child-rearing and socialization practices of different social groups. The role of language in structuring the cognitive patterns of children of different social origins has been recognized as important, and Lawton (1968) has drawn attention to the phenomenon of discontinuous socialization experienced by the working class child entering the middle class environment of the school. Sociological investigations of the school by Jackson and Marsden (1962), Jackson (1964) and Hargreaves (1967) have shown the system of norms and values through which they are ordered to be essentially middle class.

This is the conventional wisdom of British educational sociology. These are the studies and the methodological assumptions that students in universities and colleges of education are taught. Once the student is thoroughly familiar with these his intellectual socialization is complete. It will not be surprising that my first attempts at research were squarely in this tradition.

For nine months I taught English in a large comprehensive school and the research which has grown into this book really starts from that time. I began with a questionnaire study. Two hundred and twenty first-year pupils completed a brief questionnaire which I had designed mainly, I think, to prove to myself the power of the traditional variables. And I did. Significantly:

1 More low-stream (classes E and F) than high-stream (classes A and B) pupils said they would leave school as early as possible.

2 More high-stream than low-stream pupils said they were happy at school.

3 More children who said they would stay on at school said they wanted to work in clerical or professional jobs.

4 More children who said they would stay on at school said their friends would also stay on.

5 More children who said they intended to work in clerical or professional jobs stated that their friends intended to do similar work.

I learned two things from this study. The first, that children in the higher streams had higher aspirations and made friends with others like themselves, I should have already known. The second was rather less expected. These children were just twelve years old. They had been in their secondary school for less than three months before being given the questionnaire and yet already the impact of anticipatory socialization for their eventual socio-economic roles had been decisive. I concluded that if school experience had any part in this process then the primary school must be at least as important as the secondary school.

The direction my thinking was taking me was already clear. With my dissatisfaction with the existing methodologies and my belief that children's attitudes towards school learning are formed in the primary school, logic determined that I spend my first period of research in studying the contexts of learning in primary schools.

At this stage I was unaware that in the United States classroom observation is a field of its own. Much of my inspiration came from the teacher John Holt (1966 and 1970) and the anthropologist Jules Henry (1963) whose descriptions and analyses of classroom life seemed to me to be getting at the really crucial processes of the school. Both writers are concerned with the quality of the interpersonal relationship between the teacher and the pupil; how the teacher's expectations for his pupils can set up self-fulfilling prophecies so that their success or failure may be determined by the ideas she has about them, and how the implicit cultural meanings of the curriculum are transmitted. My own teaching experience showed me that in schools all was not what it seemed to be. Three incidents in particular influenced my thinking. The first alerted me to the dangers in assuming that the official perception of the school, even at the level of verifiable fact, will be accurate. The other two describe formative researches which suggested to me not only that a close examination of the contexts of learning in school were necessary but provided me with a possible research method:

1   A document issued to new members of staff in July 1969 read: 'Allocation to a class within each band (of ability) is arbitrary, and within bands, classes should be of comparable ability.' To support this theory the seven first-year classes were called 1/A1, 1/A2, 1/A3 (band A), 1/B1, 1/B2, 1/B3 (band B) and 1/C (remedial band). In fact, the mean verbal IQ scores for these seven classes proved to be: 102, 98, 94, 91, 88, 82 and 77. Had the children been banded as the school says they were the figures should have been: 98, 98, 98, 88, 88, 88, and 77. One can only conclude that the children were streamed and that, for some reason, the school did not want the fact known.

2   The parents of children about to enter the school were assured that: 'During the first two years or so a common curriculum is followed to enable transfers between streams to be made easily.' Following a 'common curriculum' usually meant that the lower stream classes copied from the blackboard notes prepared for an 'A' class in a previous lesson. At the end of the year a boy in class 1/B3 (i.e. the 'F' stream) handed in to me his geography exercise book. He had written:

NEW Foundland

Newroundland lies off the East Cost of Canada at the mouth of the St Larance River it is shaped like a tiage and ints capital city is St Johns on the East coast East of the country is an area of very shallow sea called the Grand banks a great danger to shipping round the coast rare the Icebergs which float down from Greenland between

march-and July. another danger is fog which is often found
the shortest North atlantic sea route between canada and
Europe is linked at gander Airport.

New Developments

there are two new developnients which have meant the
opening up of the country and more jods for the peopel
1. A big mining area h opened up around Benhans silver
lead zinc gold are mined
2. There is a great paper industry at corner Brook and at
Grand Falls near Cander. The forests are newsprint sent
For use all over the Americas. As a result of this opening
up of the interior a valuable farming colon is now
established behind Corner Brook conrects

How much of this the boy understood is a question best not
asked. However, we may note that his interest in what he is
doing is so low that he cannot copy correctly the words,
'coast', 'triangle', 'its', 'are', 'connects', 'developments', 'jobs',
'people', 'has', 'Gander' and 'colony'. The misspellings of the
words 'its' as 'ints', 'connects' as 'conrects' and 'development'
as 'developnient' are especially interesting since they suggest
that he copied the words precisely as he saw them on the board.
Obviously he has perceived the letter 'm' in 'development' as
'ni', a fairly simple error to make if one is merely copying as
this boy was. All in all, counting omitted and needless capitals,
missing words (possibly phrases), stops and commas, this 'copied'
piece contains forty-two errors. Lest it be thought that this was
a particularly lazy boy I will mention here that he came top
of his class at the end of the year.

3   According to the English syllabus to which I was supposed
to work my teaching was to have *limited aims*: 'full stops, capital
letters, elimination of "daisy chain" sentences; and later letters
and form filling should take priority.'
　The following areas were to be 'attacked relentlessly' throughout a child's school life:
　(a) the use of the comma instead of the full stop,
　(b) failure to indent,
　(c) failure to paragraph,

(d) failure to use capital letters properly,
(e) failure to use speech and quotation marks properly,
(f) failure to use proper headings.

The learning of grammar by rote was also advised: 'It is particularly recommended that the learning – by rote or otherwise – of the verbs mentioned in this scheme be insisted upon: this will avoid many difficulties in the higher age groups.' These things were to be 'hammered in' and 'relentless and varies' (sic) attacks on errors and 'howlers' were to be made. This programme was designed and intended to impart taste: 'We want every child to use his own judgement, to weigh evidence impartially, to discriminate between the true and the false, the meretricious and the genuine, the shoddy and the worthwhile, the transient and the eternal.' However, this sort of writing was to be deprecated: 'Ornate or "pretty-pretty" writing should be discouraged.'

I disregarded this syllabus and instead did my best to encourage the children to get all the practice they could in simply writing. It is interesting to compare the work of the boy whose geography work we have just seen with writing done out of interest:

Adventure Story

My friend Jack went on a holdiday to the sea side and enjoyed it very much. One day he made up his mind and joined the Merchant Navy as a Boy Sailor He went to Training School and then when He has passed all his exams he joined a big cargo ship. He has visited all the big ports and. life to him is a big Adventure when I am older I too would like to go to sea and Jack joined the HMS Ajax and one day a ware come and Jack was killed the ship went down and every one was killed it was the best out.

This story contains ten errors. There were another eight but he corrected those himself – he made no corrections to the copied piece. Since there are 110 words the ratio of errors to words is about 1 : 11 representing an increase in accuracy in doing his own work of more than two and a half times.

Experience, then, and much of the literature, persuaded me

that studies of children's responses to the processes of school, whether responses of learning success or failure, of adjustment or maladjustment, cannot be investigated without a personal understanding of the contexts in which these processes occur. To me it is axiomatic that the best place to carry out research into classroom learning is the classroom. With these feelings I felt it appropriate to spend my first year of research in a primary school.

Although essentially a preliminary and exploratory study – not one designed to test rigorously defined hypotheses – there were certain loosely formulated guiding presumptions which may be stated. My interest had two facets: interpersonal perception in the teacher/pupil relationship, and the classroom as a cultural system. My approach to interpersonal perception was particularly influenced by work into expectancy fulfilment and one of my first concerns was to develop a technique of revealing the ways in which teachers perceived their pupils. The method I eventually adopted will be discussed in chapter 3, but before relating this it will be best to introduce the primary school in which I spent my first research year.

Chapter 2 Children and their class positions

There were several criteria influencing the choice of a school in which to work. Principally I wanted a small, unstreamed primary school in a socially mixed area. There were two reasons for believing a small school to be most suitable; first, I wanted the study to include all children of certain ages and with the limited time available one class of each age seemed sufficient. Second, large staffs tend to split into separate groups often along lines of age, political beliefs or teaching style, and since it seemed essential to be on good terms with all teachers this was a factor that weighed quite heavily in my thinking. Co-operation from everyone in the school was essential. I intended to be in the school over a long period of time (it proved to be almost an entire school year) for sometimes four and sometimes five days a week, carrying out a programme which by its very nature required a great deal of freedom to come and go as and where I pleased without very much explanation of my precise aims. A streamed school promised to introduce complications, which were not ones I wanted to study, and which might have obscured aspects of the teachers' perceptions which were my main interest. A mixed area seemed most appropriate mainly because I had a suspicion – little more than a hunch – that with young children social class differences are difficult to identify at classroom level and that the labels 'working class' and 'middle class' perhaps acted more as 'prophecies' for later responses than as meaningful descriptions of currently present behavioural differences. It would have been impossible to test this in a school where the pupils were all from one class background.

In the event the primary school adviser for this area found me a school which fitted my requirements almost exactly. It is a small, two-storey, half-prefabricated building about fifteen years old, situated on a local authority housing estate on the southern outskirts of the city. There are approximately four hundred pupils aged between five and twelve years. The children are mainly from working class homes, but about 15 per cent have parents employed in clerical or professional occupations. The school is staffed by eleven class teachers and a headmaster. There is a full-time adjustment (remedial) teacher, a teaching auxiliary, and part-time teachers of sewing, singing, and (for part of the year) art; speech therapists and psychologists from the Child Guidance Centre are occasional visitors. The janitor and his wife are important figures and there are almost always two or three students on teaching practice so that the overall ratio of adults to children is considerably higher (and more meaningful) than the teacher/pupil ratio. Organization of the school is straightforward, there are eleven classes – four infant, seven junior – with the children grouped by age. Roughly speaking each class is six months older than the one below. Classes are normally taught by a class teacher for a period of one year, though this may be varied. The atmosphere in the school is friendly and the children are treated with tolerance and good humour by the headmaster and his staff. There is little visible enforcement of authority. Pupils wear their own clothes rather than a uniform and they chatter as they move along the corridors at their own pace. The niggling feeling of oppression one can come across in some schools is quite absent.

Fitting into the routine of the school was less difficult than I had anticipated. The headmaster was willing to provide access to records and classrooms. Class teachers were informed at the outset of the research that I was interested in observing normal children in normal lessons in a normal school. Most teachers seemed to believe this story (it was substantially true) and no one was unwilling to allow me in her classroom. Indeed the help and co-operation given me by the staff, many of whom visited the university in their own time for an interview, was essential to my research and I am most grateful to them. In several ways, by taking classes when teachers were absent, accompanying children on excursions and so on, I was able to make myself visibly useful which certainly helped in integrating myself within the school. A lot has been written of the problems experienced by participant observers in schools. It seems to me that the research student is in a particularly happy position in this respect. One's very lack of status as a mere student greatly relaxes teachers who might well be threatened by a 'research psychologist'. In the early stages, at least, my main problem was in persuading teachers that I didn't visit their classes to be instructed in teaching methods!

After a few weeks observing in the school I decided to investigate the children's awareness of their status within the class. My interest in this problem grew out of my central concern with teacher/pupil perception. The idea that a pupil's attainments and behaviour may be significantly influenced by what he perceives to be his teacher's expectations for him has been current in educational thinking – if in a rather embryonic form – for many years. But the new determination of research workers to get to grips with the problem seems to have been inspired by the relative failure of traditional methodology to demonstrate conclusively the superiority of rival systems in the teaching business. Study after study has failed to settle between the disputed pretensions of comprehensive and tripart- ite organizations, class teaching and group methods, and stream- ing and non-streaming. Indeed, Barker-Lunn's (1970) report on this last question must have disappointed the claimants and propagandists for both sides. After a thorough and massive investigation her essential conclusion was that the effects of a streamed or non-streamed classroom organization were less important in themselves than the attitudes of the teachers. In particular Barker-Lunn's work contains a salutory lesson for those who put their faith in large sample studies. Results from one half of a sample of 72 matched primary schools showed that pupils in non-streamed schools made better progress than those in streamed schools. But the other matched half showed precisely the reverse; that pupils in streamed schools did better than those in non-streamed schools. Barker-Lunn concludes that the differences must be due to some unknown factor but the implications for survey work of this 'now you see it now you don't' result are profound.

Streaming in the Primary School made several empirically supported references to the effect of teacher 'expectations' on pupil attainment. Noting that the reading performance of children of lower social class origin fell off in relation to higher social class children, the author questioned whether this was an effect wholly caused by factors of home environment (Barker-Lunn, 1970, p. 67): 'in addition it is possible that teachers' attitudes have something to do with it – the tendency for them to have lower "expectancies" for children from lower social groups.'

Barker-Lunn drew a thread of evidence in support of this suggestion from her finding that although teachers' ability ratings and children's actual performance on an English test generally agreed, of those which did not it was the lower social class children who were underestimated. In the streamed school this tendency to overestimate the upper social group and under-estimate the lower social group probably resulted in the alloca-tion of lower working class children to too low an ability stream and middle class and upper working class children to too high a stream. Similarly, in the non-streamed school, this tendency probably resulted in the development of an 'expectancy' towards the performance of pupils which will tend to be lower for lower social class children and higher for upper social class children than their actual potential. If the suggested causal relationship operates between these two findings then the con-clusion must be that underestimation of the abilities of lower working class children helps to determine their decline in performance.

Ironically, the reliance upon group tests, questionnaires and large samples has pushed educational psychology into the very area where these customary techniques can least adequately cope. A recent attempt by Pidgeon (1970) to demonstrate the effects of teacher expectations arrived at conclusions that were tentative in the extreme. The most suggestive report was of a finding by Burstall (1970) which showed that the scores of low ability children on an oral test given after two years' French teaching were not scattered randomly among the various schools in the sample but were concentrated in a small number of schools where teachers expressed negative attitudes. Burstall (quoted in Pidgeon, 1970, p. 34) concluded:

In a complex of factors determining a pupil's achievement, it must surely be recognized that the teacher's attitudes and expectations are of paramount importance. We readily accept that curriculum change cannot be effected without

the wholehearted involvement of the teachers; we are
perhaps a little less ready to recognize that changes in the
curriculum, no matter how far-reaching, will have little
effect on the pupils from whom the teacher expects – and
obtains – a low level of achievement.

The indirect nature of Pidgeon's study seems to have been
influenced by the technical deficiencies of the pioneer work by
Rosenthal and Jacobson (1968). Their report that randomly
chosen children indicated to their teachers as 'spurters' re-
sponded by gaining over the next eighteen months or so attainment and IQ increments in excess of those made by control
children, is well known. Almost as well known are the criticisms
made by Thorndike (1968) and Snow (1969) of their experi-
mental procedures. However, despite Pidgeon's wariness, direct
observation and experiment seems the only conclusive way to
demonstrate the effects of teacher's 'expectancies'. It is argued
here that what really matters in the classroom goes on in the
interaction between the teacher and the pupil. Somehow the
teacher's mental attitudes to the child are (often in spite of
herself) being communicated to him. It is careful observation
of the interactions and systematic analysis of the contexts of
learning in the classroom which will discover and perhaps
eventually measure the processes involved. My observation that
children taught in a non-streamed class were able to infer
correctly from their teacher's behaviour towards them the
relative status of each pupil in the class seemed, therefore, to be
important and worth testing.

In this school children were taught in groups. In the non-
streamed classroom group teaching is the normal and approved
method. The Plowden report (1967) advised that, in particular,
groups should be formed for 'children who have reached the
same stage in reading and computation'. But it added this
warning (Plowden report, para. 824): 'Clear cut streaming
within a class can be more damaging to children than streaming
within a school. Even from the infant school there still come too
many stories of children streamed by the table they sit at, of
"top tables" and "backward reader" tables. . . .' Barker-Lunn
(1970, p. 134) found a little empirical evidence to support
Plowden's fears:

The image a child has of himself appears also to be based on his teacher's attitude, how well he can do his school work, and how he compares with his classmates in terms of his work standard, marks and even class position. *More* boys of below average ability in streamed schools had a 'good self-image' compared with a comparable group of boys in non-streamed schools, presumably because, although they were likely to be in the lower ability stream, some of them could still be top or do the best work in their class: this being a much more unlikely feat for children in non-streamed classes.

The non-streamed classes I observed were not seated or taught in the same groups for all subjects. Following the Plowden model most teachers (six of the eight studied) seated their pupils in groups of more or less mixed ability and all had separate groups for teaching reading, number and writing. Often there were other groups formed for whatever activities the teacher thought fit.

It is interesting to compare the class in which a 'top' and a 'bottom' table were most obviously apparent with the class in which they were least apparent. Class three (pupils aged eight) was clearly 'streamed by table'. Pupils were grouped for number, writing, English and reading. The degree of congruence between the groups is shown by the Venn diagram in Figure 1(1).

It will be noted that the highest English and reading groups are composed of the same children who all sit together at the 'top table'. Three of them form the highest number group. The situation is similar in the lowest ability group. Of the seven children who sit together at the 'bottom table' six are members of the lowest reading group. Moreover, ten of the eleven pupils in the lowest reading group form the whole of the lowest English group.

Class eight (pupils aged eleven) was very differently arranged. Again a Venn diagram is helpful. This teacher formed only two teaching groups (number and English) and made sure that the seating pattern did not reflect these groups. Thus we see from Figure 1(2) that although half of the highest number group are members of the highest English group they do not sit at the 'top table'. In fact, only half of the children at this table are

Figure 1 *Venn diagrams showing the degree of overlap between teaching groups*

(1) *In a class of eight-year-olds*

(a) Highest ability groups

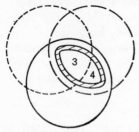

Total 7

(b) Lowest ability groups

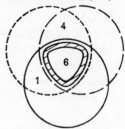

Total 11

(2) *In a class of eleven-year-olds*

(a) Highest ability groups

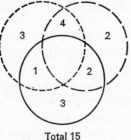

Total 15

(b) Lowest ability groups

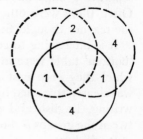

Total 12

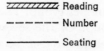

///////// Reading

------ Number

——— Seating

— — — English

members of either the highest number group or the highest English group. In the lowest ability group a similar dispersion exists. Here the 'bottom table' (if we may fairly call it such) contains only one pupil from each of the lowest number and English groups. Note also that two of the three children in the lowest number group are also members of the lowest English group.

As practised by this teacher, the group teaching method could scarcely have been bettered. In spite of this, however, her pupils were still able to tell exactly which group was higher than another and which children were better or worse than they.

An extract from a tape-recorded interview with four eleven-year-old girls will illustrate this:

RN What groups are you in, Jane?

J The purple group, the red group, and the blue group.

RN Take the purple group, what's that for?

J Sitting

RN Ah, just by seats. What's the next one?

J The red group's for sums.

RN The red group's for sums. Now are any of you others in the same group as Jane?

J Christine and Carol are in the red group and in the blue English group.

RN Carol and Christine are in the same groups as you. And what groups are you in then?

S The purple group for sitting.

RN And what sum group?

S The green sum group.

RN Is that a higher or a lower one?

S It's another one. She's . . . the red group's the top group.

RN I see, you do easier sums, do you?

S Yes.

RN Now what English group are you in?

S The yellow.

RN You're in the yellow English group. Who else here is in the yellow English group with you?

S No one.

RN So you're mainly in groups for sitting, for sums and . . . ?

All children For reading.

RN What are the reading groups then?

S Yellow, pink, green, and blue.

RN Now you can tell me about that, Christine. Who's in the same group as you?

Ch Jane and Carol.

RN   Again? So you're the same . . . ?
Ch   Us three are always in the same groups.
s   Except they're not in the same sitting.

It looks most confusing, but these girls knew just what groups there were, knew which were the highest and which the lowest, and knew who was in each group. One of the implications of this struck me with especial force when a six-year-old remarked boastfully of a classmate, 'She's not so clever as me. I'm on book six.' Her friend was on book five and in a lower group. It is a very simple piece of reasoning.

If book two is higher than book one, and if it's true that children who read better are the cleverer, then when Joan is on book two and Susan is on book one, the conclusion must be that Joan is more clever than Susan. Once children know which group is higher than another, the same is true of groups. Joan knows she is more clever than Susan – and so does Susan. Whatever else children may learn or fail to learn at school, they learn this – to measure themselves against their classmates. It is just possible for a child to leave school unable to read. But it is inconceivable that he should be unaware that this puts him at the bottom of the list. There is a sense, therefore, in which it can be said that schools teach heirarchical levels of personal worth more successfully than anything else. The child in school is in a position where the teacher and the other children all, by their relationships with him, place him in certain positions with respect to themselves and oblige him to take up certain roles. From these positions and roles he must build up his ideas of who he is. In such a manner is the schoolchild's self-image fashioned.

Suspecting this I set out to establish precisely how accurate children's perceptions of their class positions were. First of all I obtained from three teachers rank orders of ability on three measures; number, writing, and reading, for the children in their classes. Each child was then seen individually and asked to point to the names, written on cards arranged randomly on the desk before him, of the 'people a wee bit better than you at number'. The same procedure was followed for testing whom the child thought better than himself at reading and writing. From these data it was possible to estimate each child's self-perceived class position. For example, if a child pointed to ten children as a' wee bit better' than himself, he was assumed to regard his position in the class as eleventh. It is necessary to be quite clear about what was happening here. The teachers' rankings were made at my request and were not communicated to their pupils. In theory the children should have had no idea of their class positions and had I directly asked children what their positions were I suspect I should have got some strange answers. But tested in this indirect way children aged as young as eight gave themselves positions which correlated

Table 1 *Correlations between teachers' ranks on school subjects and pupils' own estimates of their positions*

Age	Reading	Writing	Number	Totals	N
8	0·69	0·44	0·64	0·85	28
10	0·31	0·20*	0·45	0·46	30
11	not applicable	0·47	0·80	0·82	33

Note: The totals in this table have been made by summing the individual scores and ranking the totals. For example, a child who gave himself the following positions; reading tenth, writing eighth, and number thirteenth, would receive a score of thirty-one. If, when this figure was ranked with the others, its rank proved to be ninth, that would be regarded as his 'total' or overall class position. This would then be correlated with the totals similarly derived from the individual perceptions given him by his teacher. All correlations are Kendall's Tau and, with the single exception of the asterisked figure, are significant at the 0·01 level.

highly with those assigned them by their teacher. The complete figures are given in Table 1.

It is interesting to see that although pupils from all classes were good at this exercise, the 'streamed' eight-year-olds were better than at least one of the older 'non-streamed' classes. The ten-year-olds were certainly less able at estimating their positions than the eight-year-olds. The eleven-year-olds *were* slightly better than the eight-year-olds, but this could well have been due to their greater sophistication. They were three years older. The arrangement of the groups in the class of ten-year-olds was similar to that in the class of eleven-year-olds.

As a result of this it is reasonable to ask if the attempt to disguise from children their class positions is worthwhile. It seems a pointless mystification to call teaching groups by colours or animals when children are, in fact, aware of their real status. Certainly the technique is not enough to prevent children gaining knowledge of the relative abilities within the class. Perhaps one should not make too much of this. The ages of the children are not comparable and three classes is a small sample. Nevertheless, these results seem worth following up.

Rosenthal and Jacobson (1968) reported the findings of a study in which it was shown that subjects wanted to have their expectancies fulfilled to such an extent that they preferred bad news to good if it was bad news they were expecting. Perhaps children, even those with low positions, expect these positions to be confirmed and so may even learn to prefer these positions?

If so, then this research has some interesting implications. The assumption that children strive to maintain their relative status within the class for the sake of personal consistency makes some sense. Can it be that the position you know is better than the position you don't? Once children have firmly accepted their position with respect to their classmates perhaps they not only do not attempt to alter it but adapt their learning responses to keep it constant. Experiments by Asch, described by Brown (1965), have demonstrated the power of group pressure to alter considerably even the perception of visual stimuli. These experiments, in which subjects were shown lines, the lengths of which they had to guess after hearing the guesses of the experimenters accomplices who *all* lied about their estimates, may have some relevance to the classroom problem I am concerned with. Most of Asch's subjects went along with the stooges' highly inaccurate guesses.

Certainly, a child who believes he is somewhere in the middle of the class, but not as clever as Tommy, Sarah, Johnny and the rest of the group, will probably not strive to outshine them. Similarly, if he also believes that he is not as slow as Freddy, Joan, Billy and their group he will probably try to keep above them. Sociologists (for example, Klein, 1965) have described a similar mechanism operating between the 'rough' and the 'respectable' sections within working class society. The 'respectables' do all they can *not* to be associated with the 'roughs' who, in their turn, are keen not to be confused with their 'respectable' neighbours whom they typically regard as 'stuck up'. Each group maintains its position by investing divergent cultural habits with a ritual significance to denote its separateness from the other group. So children in the classroom may use their knowledge of their relative positions in ways which act to maintain their status.

Chapter 3 Teachers' perceptions of their pupils

So far I had discovered that children were aware of their relative abilities within the classroom and found at least some evidence that this awareness was related to their teacher's grouping methods. It has been well established, by Barker-Lunn (1970) among others, that a teacher's grouping practices reflect her general attitudes towards teaching and education. My work was thus approaching what I regard as the central problem of classroom research: do the teacher's attitudes towards her pupils influence their performance in school? In the previous chapter I examined several researches, Barker-Lunn (1970), Pidgeon (1970), Burstall (1970), and Rosenthal and Jacobson (1968), which were concerned with what has become known as the 'expectancy' problem.

These studies have tackled a hitherto neglected area. However, all the research into this subject has been carried out from the empiricist standpoint described in chapter 1. It has all been concerned with the overall effects, on large groups of children, of teachers' attitudes to styles of teaching; for example, to streaming, or 'permissiveness'. None has so far attempted to measure directly the attitudes of individual teachers to individual pupils.

It seemed to me that in order to discover whether the school performance of individual children was influenced by their teacher's attitudes towards them, some measure of the teacher's attitudes to each child in her class was needed. A very powerful method of exploring such individual constructs has been made available by George Kelly's Personal Construct Theory. Although originally developed for clinical use the repertory grid technique associated with this theory has been increasingly employed in research. In this country Bannister and Mair (1968) have reported several different applications and refinements of method. The core of Kelly's theory assumes that each individual views the significant events and people in his life through a repertoire of personal bi-polar constructs. The theory suggests that if we want to know what attitudes a person holds we should make it our task to discover what these actually *are*, rather than, as is conventionally done, ask him to agree or disagree with a list of statements somehow held to form a 'scale'. So if we want to investigate the relationship between a teacher's attitudes to her pupils and those pupils' behaviour it is more meaningful to discover what are the teacher's constructs than impose upon her an 'attitude test' constructed by the researcher.

I decided to employ the repertory grid to discover what constructs were held by the teachers in the research school towards the children in their classes. All eight junior school teachers (infant teachers were omitted) agreed to go through the procedure. The eight classes amounted to 236 pupils.

The great attraction of personal construct theory lies in its close association with practice. With the teachers I used the original triadic elicitation procedure. The teacher is presented with three cards each bearing the name of one of her pupils and asked to group together the two which seem in some respect to be most alike. She might, for example, say that two are noisy and the third very quiet. Thus the bi-polar construct *Quiet – Noisy* is obtained. Ten or twelve constructs are elicited and ranked by the teacher according to the direction, 'If you were taking over a new class which piece of information would you find most useful?' The purpose of this is to rank the constructs according to their importance as she sees it. Finally, in order to establish which pole of the construct is preferred by the teacher she is asked, 'In general are children towards this or that end of the construct most likely to succeed at school?' The eight most highly ranked constructs are taken as a fair measure of the average teacher's repertoire and are converted to a rating scale. A four-point scale is used, for example, 1 Quiet, 2 tends to Quietness, 3 tends to Noisiness, and 4 Noisy. Each child in the class is rated on each of the eight constructs. The resulting figures are then rank-ordered, ties being eliminated by giving within each set of ties a higher rank to those children scoring higher on the constructs defined by the teacher as more important. The children with the lowest scores are assumed to be those most favourably perceived and those with the highest scores to be the least favourably perceived. The lowest possible score is eight, and the highest thirty-two. The pupils were ranked on this measure and each child's position noted. This position will be called construct rank. It may be valuable at this point to provide a concrete example of the grid procedure. Let us suppose the teacher has rated four children on her eight constructs and that the scores are as shown:

Constructs	1	2	3	4	5	6	7	8	Sum
Mark	1	2	1	2	2	1	3	1	13
John	4	3	4	1	3	4	2	2	23
Peter	2	1	2	2	1	1	1	3	13
Paul	4	4	3	3	3	4	3	4	28

It will be seen that the scores received by Mark and Peter both run to 13. In ranking the tie is eliminated by giving Mark the higher rank on the ground that he obtains a higher score on the first construct. The constructs have been ordered by the teacher in terms of their importance. The construct ranks of these four boys are thus: Mark 1, Peter 2, John 3, and Paul 4. Suppose that this teacher's first three constructs are: 1 *Quiet – Noisy*, 2 *Mature – Immature*, and 3 *Hardworking – Lazy*. It is argued here that the teacher perceives Mark as: *Quiet*, tending to be *Mature*, and *Hardworking*. By contrast it is argued that she perceives John as: *Noisy*, tending to be *Immature*, and *Lazy*. In later applications of the repertory grid to teachers a six-point scale was substituted in place of the four-point scale used here.

This test was given independently to eight teachers and obviously the constructs they used varied in detail. However, there was a surprising agreement among them about what may be called 'core constructs'. Three distinct constructs were found in most teachers' responses. These are shown in Table 2.

The three most common constructs were *Hardworking – Lazy, Mature – Immature*, and *Well behaved – Poorly behaved*. There were slight variations in the wording of these constructs, for example, a teacher might express *Hardworking – Lazy* as *Tries hard – Slacks*, or by some similar phrase; however, their communality was obvious. One is immediately struck by the variation

in the ranks given to these constructs, implying how important the teachers consider them. There is agreement among six
teachers that *Hardworking – Lazy* is important, they place it
among the first four. Two teachers, on the other hand, place it
seventh. *Mature – Immature* seems to bring out the most disagreement. Two teachers say that it is the most important factor of
all, yet two others place it sixth and seventh. Five is the modal
rank. There is more agreement about the *Well behaved – Poorly
behaved* construct. Two teachers place it least in importance, and
none place it among the first three. The modal rank is six.

From this evidence we are entitled to say that the junior
school teachers in this school perceived their pupils primarily in

Table 2 *The three most frequently used constructs with the ranking allotted
them by eight primary school teachers*

Construct	Teacher								
	A	B	C	D	E	F	G	H	Mode
Hardworking – Lazy	2	2	7	4	1	2	7	4	2
Mature – Immature	5	1	3	1	6	7	5	5	5
Well behaved – Poorly behaved	6	8	4	5	4	5	6	6	6

terms of their work habits, their maturity, and their classroom
behaviour. All the constructs related to aspects of the child's
personality. It is very interesting to note that none deal
specifically with the child's abilities. The *Hardworking – Lazy*
construct describes the effort the child puts into his work, not
his ability to do it. From these teachers I only occasionally
elicited constructs such as *Bright – Dull, Does good work – Does
poor work*, and *High IQ – Low IQ* which I later found from other
primary school teachers.

This school has a local reputation for being 'progressive' and
'child-centred'. The investigation of the teachers' constructs by
means of the repertory grid technique seems to have supported
the claims upon which this reputation is based. The teachers
appear to think of, and to judge, their pupils not mainly in
terms of their academic ability but by the personality attributes
they regard as important to good progress in school.

Knowing the constructs with which each teacher perceived her pupils enabled the observations I made of pupils' classroom behaviour to be examined in the teacher's own terms. In the following pages the observations of the behaviour of two eight-year-old boys in the same class are presented together with some analysis. John has a high construct rank; he is favourably perceived by the teacher, George has a low construct rank; he is unfavourably perceived. The observations were made consecutively on the same morning.

Observation record 1   John

9.30   The teacher is testing the children's ability to tell the time. She holds a large wooden clock face with movable hands set at nine o'clock. 'What do you do at that time?' she asks. A boy answers, 'I come to school!' John calls out, 'I go to my bed at nine o'clock.' The teacher moves the hands several times and always John raises his hand eager to answer. 'How many minutes past twelve?' asks the teacher. A boy gets up

9.42   for some reason and blocks John's view, 'I canna see!' he calls. At the end of the lesson the teacher tells the class to work from their cards on their own. John is learning about birds. On the workcard prepared by his teacher are several sketches of birds' heads and a paragraph setting a task:

> You don't see many birds with heads like this. Why do you think a duck has a beak like this? What kind of food might it eat?

John takes from his desk two large books about birds and turns to the illustrations. He shows his neighbour a photograph of an owl holding a mouse in its claws. He tells him how his father had 'found a mouse and put it in a box but it was dead'. He chatters almost ceaselessly as he draws an owl, closely copying the book illustration. After a few minutes the teacher, who is hearing groups of children read at her desk, calls him out with his neighbour to hear them read. He is slightly above average in his reading ability. After this he returns to his desk and looks at the drawings of birds he has made in his book; they are neat and carefully coloured with crayon pencil. The teacher now instructs the class to put away their work books and workcards and John replaces his in their proper place. The next lesson is hand-work. John goes to the 'craft table' and searches through the piles of cigarette packets and eggboxes for his model. He cannot find it and complains to the teacher. She realizes that it must have been thrown away in error by the new cleaner and explains to John what has happened. John looks a bit sad at this news. The teacher says he can help her and she sends him off to make some glue. He pours out a little glue powder into a tin lid and carries it out to the washroom to mix it with water. When he returns the teacher says he can help her make a frieze. First the teacher pins a drawing of his done on a previous day to the wall and John dances impatiently while she searches in her desk for pins. Then he goes to the back, takes a BBC pamphlet which is hanging on the wall and brings it to the teacher's desk. He stands there at the corner tracing a picture of a camel. He shows her the result talking all the time. He discusses with the teacher how best to arrange the tracing on a sheet of paper. Carefully John goes over the tracing transferring the outline on to the red paper. 'Let's see,' asks his teacher. John chatters as he cuts out the camel he has drawn. 'I don't know how I'm going to get the camel on,' he says. The teacher suggests that he should stick it with glue and they talk for a minute or so about different sorts of glue and sticky paper. Finally the camel is cut out. John 'walks' it over the teacher's desk. 'What shall I do now, Miss?' he asks.

10.03

10.15

Analysis

John is seen favourably by his teacher as *Vivacious, Mature, Demanding of attention, Able to be left alone, Of high ability*, and unfavourably as, tending to be *Poorly behaved, Noisy*, and *A gang member*. It is possible to examine John's observed behaviour in terms of these constructs.

Favourable constructs

Vivacious: a particularly idiosyncratic construct this. But note John's constant talking, and, perhaps, the way he plays with his teacher, 'walking' the camel over her desk.

Mature: observe how he takes the news that his model has been destroyed. He does not sulk or show any temper. For a few moments he looks sad but accepts the task his teacher gives instead and does it cheerfully. This sort of maturity is probably what the teacher has in mind.

Demanding of attention: this is fairly apparent. He works with the teacher at her desk for nearly fifteen minutes and several times previously occupied her attention.

Able to be left alone: at first seemingly contradictory to the previous construct but if we note the way he carries out several tasks, for example, preparing the glue and obtaining the right sort of paper from the cupboard, we can get some idea of what the teacher presumably means.

Of high ability: note particularly the way he realizes that nine o'clock comes round twice a day. 'I go to my bed at nine o'clock!' he says in response to a boy who has given the expected answer, 'At nine o'clock I come to school.' Note also that his work is neat and that no errors are observed.

Unfavourable constructs

A gang member: it really isn't possible to observe this in the record. Sociometric data shows him, however, to have many friends in the class.

Noisy: clearly his constant talking is to blame for this.

Tending to be Poorly behaved: perhaps the way he calls out without raising his hand and the uninhibited way he protests that he 'canna see' when someone blocks his view indicates why the teacher sees him on just the wrong side of the *Well behaved – Poorly behaved* construct.

Observation record 2   George

11.03   George is writing the news. The class have discussed the events of recent days and the teacher has written difficult words and phrases on the board, 'Student Charities Parade', 'Satellite', 'Commonwealth Games'. George's writing is untidy, his spelling poor, many of his letters are reversed, and though he uses a basically i.t.a. script he is apt to muddle in traditional ortho-graphy at apparently random intervals. All in all it is impossible for me to make out what he is writing. Later his teacher helps me to decipher it. It says:

> When I went to London I saw
> town at London the town
> he saw cat in the town the
> town the cat's name was Sam

11.24 I ask George to read his writing to me but he can read only odd words and is unable to give any sensible narra-tive. It has taken him twenty minutes to do this. There have been interruptions to collect the dinner money and call the register, but he has been writing more or less steadily. At the end of this session the teacher tells the class to place their books in a pile on a table near the door and tells them to choose a book to read from the 'library'. George seems restless and unable to settle down. He leaves his seat five times to fetch a book from the shelves. He treats each in the same way, not turning over the pages singly but opening the book at four or five places and looking at the pictures where there are any. Occasionally a picture captures his attention and he shows it to his neighbour, 'Look India. There's India,' he says pointing to an illustration of a cowboy.

11.32 After this session the teacher hands out to the pupils their writing books. George goes to the front to sharpen his pencil at the machine on the teacher's desk. The teacher asks him, rather sharply, where he got his pencil from. George replies that it is a school pencil. 'Not one of my school pencils,' says the teacher, 'I've got blue ones.' George looks unhappily at his pink

11.34 pencil. The teacher turns away to attend to someone else. George returns to his seat. The teacher asks the class to call out words containing the letter 't' and she writes their answers on the board in i.t.a. script. George watches her write up the words. He does not suggest any. He copies into his book, 'teeth', 'settee', 'kettle', 'table', 'tea'. He does this accurately but for writing 'teea' which he notices and erases with a rubber. But on the second line he reverses the curve of the letter 't' in every word. He continues like this writing out the row of words three times. Eventually the teacher asks to see his book; she is not pleased. 'Now George, which way do they go, "t"s?' George looks very crestfallen and makes a sign with his finger. 'Well, don't you write them any other way. Go and write them correctly.' He writes another line of words, 'teeth', 'settee', 'kettle', 'table', 'tea'. Every 't' is again reversed. The

11.52   teacher doesn't get the chance to see this for it is milk time. George goes out to the front with the rest of the class to get his milk and returns with it to his seat. He seems quite animated now and talks to his neighbour. He shuffles the milk carton over the desk and sticks the damp label to his forehead. He looks pleased and smiles and pulls at his neighbour's arm to show him.

Analysis

George is perceived in generally unfavourable terms by his teacher as, tending to be *Subdued*, *Immature*, *Undemanding of Attention*, *Unable to be left alone*, *Of low ability*, tending to be *Noisy*, and tending to be *Poorly behaved*, and in favourable terms as, *Independent*. George's behaviour will be examined using these constructs:

Unfavourable constructs

Tending to be Subdued: we may get some idea of what the teacher means by this construct by observing his reactions to her questions. He answers neither of them directly. In fact he addresses only one sentence to the teacher throughout the observation period. He simply looks rather puzzled at her enquiry about his pencil and draws in the air with his finger when she asks him how he should write his letters.

Immature: the teacher probably has George's overall behaviour in mind in making this judgment. His reluctance to speak to her, for example. His speech patterns, too, seem rather babyish, 'Look India. There's India', is not a meaningful statement in response to a picture of a cowboy. Nor is the way he looks through the books, opening them without apparent interest and in no ordered way, evidence of maturity.

Undemanding of attention: we have already noted that George does not seek to be noticed by the teacher. He will not ask for help except on rare occasions and we do not see him do so here.

Unable to be left alone: although George does not demand attention the teacher clearly does not feel able to leave him on his own. His work is very poor and he is not able to cope at all successfully with the demands of the classroom. The teacher presumably believes that if he is left alone he will only make more mistakes.

Of low ability: his writing alone is sufficient evidence of his poor ability and attainment.

Tending to be Noisy: it is not at all clear why this construct is applied to George. It may just be possible that the sort of behaviour we noted in his interaction with his neighbour is responsible for his being placed on just the wrong side of the *Quiet – Noisy* construct.

Tending to be Poorly behaved: George's interaction with his neighbour may be illustrative of this construct also. It is not likely that the teacher will be friendly towards behaviour of this kind, particularly if it is part of a regular pattern.

Favourable constructs

Independent: this merely means that he isn't what this teacher regards as a *Gang member.* This is not easy to see from the observation record but sociometric data shows him to have no friends in the class.

These two observations and analyses have been given to illustrate the power of the repertory grid technique: first, the constructs used by the teacher in her perception of her pupils were obtained; second, the bi-polar constructs were converted to a rating scale and a rank order on this measure of all the pupils in her class was obtained; third, the child in the classroom was observed as objectively as possible and finally, his behaviour was reinterpreted as it seemed to be perceived by his teacher. This may seem a lengthy procedure, and certainly the data is less than concise; however, the analysis of pupils' behaviour in the classroom is an important problem and this approach seems worthwhile. It might be very interesting, for example, to present teachers with video-tape recordings of the behaviour of certain of their pupils and ask them to do the interpretation. In that way we really would know what sorts of behaviour the teacher perceived in favourable or unfavourable terms.

If the attitude and perceptions of the teacher do influence pupils' behaviour this looks a promising way of finding out. Pidgeon (1970) indicates two ways in which this process might take place: (i) if a teacher regards work as above the pupil she will not teach it, and, (ii) if a pupil is led to believe he is capable of little he will have low expectations of himself, little motivation, and will, in fact, achieve little. The second procedure is the more interesting psychologically. This study was made in a primary school where the children in each class are taught by a single teacher. In secondary school, by contrast, the children will be taught by perhaps a dozen teachers. All these teachers will perceive the children in their own individual way and the children will similarly perceive their teachers differently. Using the methods described above it ought to be possible to show how children modify their behaviour in response to the way they are perceived by their teachers. This will be the subject of later chapters.

Chapter 4 Social measures and classroom measures

In my first chapter I discussed briefly the finding of the educational sociologists that low social class and low ability go hand-in-hand. The two following chapters discussed the outcome of my researches into a different area; the effects of teacher attitudes in determining pupils' school progress. Here I wish to draw the two aspects together.

We may hypothesize that if teacher attitudes are important determinants of ability the rank order derived from the repertory grid should correlate more highly with ability than does social class. Accordingly, social class data, obtained from the school records and coded on the five-point scale used by Barker-Lunn (1970), was correlated with two ability measures: a reading quotient obtained from scores on the Schonell R3 Reading Test, and the class teacher's estimate of ability expressed as a rank. It should be noted that though social class data was obtained from five classes it was only possible to administer the reading test to four. The coefficients of correlation, from Downie and Heath (1970), were both statistically non-significant:

Social class – Reading Quotient   r. = 0·10   N. 110
Social class – Class Position   r. = 0·15   N. 144

However, correlations calculated between construct rank and the ability measures were significant at the 0·05 level:

Construct rank – Reading Quotient r. = 0·31   N. 107
Construct rank – Class Position   r. = 0·36   N. 144

This is surely a noteworthy finding. It seems that whereas social class is of dubious relationship to ability and attainment within a class of children, the way those children are perceived by their teacher certainly is not. These results are the more surprising for social background has been regarded for more than a decade as the major factor determining school ability. Among the more important studies which have emphasized this are Douglas (1964), and the follow-up study Douglas, Ross and Simpson (1968), Ford (1970), and Lawton (1968). Douglas is interested in large-scale survey work, Ford is a sociological theorist and Lawton is interested in language. Each has a different approach; but the overall picture they give is of working class children handicapped by lack of parental interest, low aspirations, attitudes unfavourable to

Table 3　*The constructs held by one primary teacher towards two of her pupils and their scores on a four-point scale*

Construct scales	Jamie	Robert
Forthcoming – Emotionally disturbed	1	3
Easy-going – Worrier	1	4
Industrious – Lazy	1	3
Confident – Lacks confidence	1	3
Interested – Lacks interest	1	2
Quiet – Talkative	1	4
Boisterous – Shy	1	3
Bright – Dull	1	3

learning and difficulties with language. There is a heavy sense of inevitability about it all. And therein lies the danger.

It was suggested earlier that what really matters in the class-room lies in the interaction between the teacher and the pupil. In one way or another the teacher's mental attitudes are communicated to him. There is no real mystery about this process, though the methodological constraints we impose upon ourselves make it difficult to observe systematically. Children are very quick, for example, to notice when a teacher is making 'pets' – and so is the classroom observer. But he has to work to higher degrees of certainty than they. He can count the number of times the teacher smiles at different children, measure the amount of time she spends with them, note the kind of praise she gives, the tone of voice she uses and so on. I say he *can*. But while he sits there counting smiles or whatever, he is ignoring just about everything else that is going on. However, if one is prepared to accept a more phenomenological approach it is not difficult to understand how some children learn that the teacher doesn't think much of them. Table 3 shows the constructs of one primary teacher towards two of her pupils. From this information it is possible to see that the teacher regards Jamie in more favourable terms than Robert. Jamie she sees as: *Forthcoming, Easy-going, Industrious, Confident, Interested, Quiet, Boisterous,* and *Bright.* Robert is perceived as: *A worrier, Talkative,* and tending to be *Emotionally disturbed, Lazy, Lacking confidence, Shy,* and *Low IQ.* His one good point is that he tends to be *Interested.*

The two following records were made of the boys' classroom behaviour. It will be interesting to compare them.

Observation record 3   Robert

> Most of the class are doing project work. Three boys still seem to be doing English. This means they haven't finished quickly enough. Teacher looks over to them. 'Robert, you could be doing an excellent drawing for me but you're so slow with your English.' Robert looks glum. He puts down his pencil. Looks like he's finished at last – or given up. He goes to the teacher who is telling Albert what a 'lovely wee campfire' he has painted. She sees Robert standing a bit behind her not drawing attention to himself. 'Ah, now you can help me here,' she says. She heads him over to the model tray. 'We're going to have the Rockies either side and that's going to be a wee pass. Are you very good at making mountain shapes?' Robert looks doubtfully at the heap of papier mâché. 'No?' asks the teacher. 'Well, I'll get someone else to do that then.' She tells him to do a picture instead. Robert goes back to his desk. He looks about, sees that he hasn't any paper to draw on and decides to finish his English. A couple of minutes later teacher asks the class, 'Anyone still doing English?' Robert raises his hand. 'Oh, come on, Robert,' she says.

That's just ten minutes. Most of Robert's time at school seems to be like that. It is not necessary to analyse the record in any great detail to make the point that Robert appears

unhappy and unsuccessful in school. But note that the organization of the classroom is such that he is kept writing while
nearly everyone else is drawing and painting, that when he
eventually tries to get something more interesting to do the
teacher first offers him a job and in the next breath takes it
away, presumably because she believes he will make a mess of
it. Next she gives him work he can't do because he hasn't got
the materials and, finally, she gets irritated with him because
he is so slow with his English. The teacher's unfavourable
perceptions of Robert set up expectations for him so that
'laziness', 'lack of confidence', and so on are taken for granted.
This sad record may be compared with a very different one
of Jamie's life in the classroom.

Observation record 4   Jamie

Jamie is at the teacher's desk. He talks to Ian who has
just got up. They compare their work. John, in front
of Jamie, joins in. They talk energetically but in
lowered voices. Jamie watches the teacher closely as
she marks John's book. He refers to his book and makes
several alterations, corrections I expect, with his pencil.
Teacher takes his book. 'Right', she says. Then, 'Some
of you are not using very sharp pencils. I can hardly
read it.' Quickly she corrects his work. 'Jamie, there
you are.' Jamie takes his book and goes over to the
box to replace his workcard. He returns to his desk.
He flicks through his record book and ticks off the
answers. One of the boys in the queue asks him a
question and Jamie pauses to answer and talks to him
for a few moments. The teacher asks who is talking.
'I just can't concentrate with this noise whoever it is,'
she says. Jamie continues with his work. The class
quieten down. There are about twenty people now
around the teacher's desk. The noise grows louder
again. The teacher warns the class adding, 'Shirley, I
don't want that shrieking.' Jamie works quietly for
three or four minutes until the teacher has marked most
of the books. She gives up half-way through and tells
everyone to sit down. The class are now given instruc-

tions about the project they are to do. Everybody is going to write diaries of a Western pioneer family. 'I'm going to put you in families. Husbands and wives – there's no need to be silly about it – and children.' She looks round to see who has finished the English work. 'Right,' she says, 'Jamie, you pick your waggon.' Jamie grins and stands up and makes great play over picking his friends who move over to his desk.

Jamie, we see, is treated a little differently from Robert. There are no signs of open favouritism. But let us look between the lines. His speed with his work means, because of the way the classroom is organized, that he has only a minute or two to wait in the queue thus giving him a chance to complete his record book, for which he will, in time, be rewarded. Note also – and this is very important – that when his pencil is blunt and his talking disturbs the teacher she generalizes her comments to the rest of the class without mentioning his name. The teacher knows full well that Jamie was talking but she says, 'I just can't concentrate with this noise *whoever* it is.' When the chatter of a less favoured child, in this case Shirley, disturbs her the culprit is warned *by name*. In the eyes of the class Shirley is 'told off'; Jamie isn't. Finally, he is given first choice in the enjoyable business of choosing a 'family'. A substantial reward.

It needs to be stressed, I think, that the teacher will be quite unaware that she is discriminating against Robert (or Shirley) and favouring Jamie. She is certainly not consciously biased. But we have seen that she believes Jamie is highly capable and that Robert is not. Having these beliefs it would be strange if she did not act upon them.

In the early 1950s when Hertfordshire altered its eleven-plus selection procedure by substituting teachers' assessments in place of IQ tests the proportion of working class children gaining grammar school places fell and the proportion of middle class children rose. It is argued by Floud and Halsey (1957) that the teachers here proved to be an even less fair measure of ability than the IQ test. If teachers generally do have a bias against children from lower working class backgrounds it may well be strengthened by sociological studies which stress the disadvantages of coming from such a background. Indeed these surveys are all too easily interpreted by teachers as repeating what they have always known – that working class children do not do well in school and that there is little the school can do about it.

In the present study there arose a rather subtle way of testing this bias. We saw in the previous chapter that the most common constructs used by the teachers in my research school were, *Well behaved – poorly behaved, Hardworking – lazy*, and *Mature – immature*. However, four teachers also gave the construct *Good home – poor home* and thus provided a subjective measure which we may call *perceived social class*. Table 4 shows that although there is no statistically significant relationship

Table 4   *Associations between actual and perceived social class and between these and two other measures of ability*

	χ^2	d.f.	p.	N
Actual social class – Ability criterion	7·8	6	N.S.	112
Actual social class – Reading Quotient	2·2	1	N.S.	57
Perceived social class – Ability criterion	36·7	6	0·001	123
Perceived social class – Reading Quotient	5·3	1	0·05	57
Perceived social class – Actual social class	10·1	6	N.S.	117

Note: The χ^2 test for two independent samples was used here. Only for two teachers' classes were both Reading Quotients and perceived social class data available.

between actual social class and ability the relationship between *perceived social class* and ability is high.

There are two ability measures: (i) a Reading Quotient derived from the Schonell R3 Reading Test and (ii) the teacher's judgments of ability taken from her constructs elicited by the repertory grid procedure; this is called the ability criterion. There are also two measures of social class: (i) actual social class derived from the school records and coded on a five-point scale and (ii) perceived social class taken from the teacher's constructs.

The correlations between actual social class and both ability measures are not significant. However, perceived social class is significantly correlated with both ability measures. It is not simply a matter of one construct measure being necessarily correlated with another.

Once again we see that the subjective ideas of the teacher are more important than sociological reality. In order to find the relationship we have come to expect between ability and social class it is necessary to use a subjective rather than an objective measure. The teachers' judgments about home background have more to do with her pupils' behaviour and ability than with actual social class. That there was no significant correlation between actual and perceived social class need not surprise us; Goodacre (1968) found similar results. Indeed, Goodacre found that teachers' estimates were least reliable in the lowest social areas and suggested that teachers might be unfamiliar with the degrees of responsibility or training involved in manual occupations. There seem to be two possible explanations for these findings: (a) that teachers so strongly associate the ideas of low ability and low social class that they see badly behaved and dull children as being from poor homes regardless of any objective criteria; and (b) that in making judgments teachers take into account other information about the home which is only poorly estimated by socio-economic data. Both explanations probably have some truth.

That sociologists should concentrate upon demographic variables like social class is understandable; but their conclusions are open to misinterpretation by practising teachers. In fact, they may have precisely the opposite effects on teachers' behaviour from those intended. All her reading leads the teacher to accept that social class is the major factor determining the behaviour, attitudes and attainment of her pupils but this now seems less than the whole story. The fact is that at classroom level correlations with social class are very hard to find. For example, Hargreaves (1967), in his study of social relations in a secondary school, was unable to correlate allocation to stream with social class and decided, weakly, that his sample (of 100) was too small. If we have a sample of 5,000 then we may very well find correlations, but when we look more closely at smaller samples, they tend in practice to disappear. If social class is relevant to the teacher then we ought to be able to find correlations with samples of thirty. Teachers do not yet take classes of 5,000.

Liam Hudson (1966) wrote that a teacher faced with a class

of clever boys would learn little from their IQ scores. I think we can say the same about social class – and we need not limit ourselves to clever boys. Certainly children of low social origin do poorly at school; because they lack encouragement at home, because they use language in a different way from their teachers, because they have their own attitudes to learning, and so on; but *also* because of the expectations their teachers have for them. The sociological factors of which we have become so aware do not act in a vacuum; they are mediated through the interaction between the teacher and the child and the quality of these interactions depends, in part, on how favourably or unfavourably the teacher perceives the child. Social class seems to be almost irrelevant to teachers: when samples are class sized it correlates neither with objective nor with subjective measures of ability. But some teachers are so convinced that social class must be important that they perceive this correlation to exist even when it manifestly does not.

Chapter 5   The development of a research plan

During the year I spent in my initial research school my thinking had progressed beyond the stage of simple uneasiness with conventional methods in educational sciences. It was becoming clear that some degree of theoretical and methodological sophistication was needed. In the course of research I had become interested in several areas of theoretical import-ance, in particular, participant observation, personal construct theory, and symbolic interactionism. It is not my purpose in this account to produce a synthesis of these positions. I want only to discuss their importance to the development of my own thinking.

In Britain participant observation has not, until very recently, been a method much favoured by social psychologists and the American studies by, for example, McCall and Simmons (1969), and Becker (1970), have not been required reading for students. So it happened that I was busy as a participant observer some time before I caught up with the literature. Though I was convinced that the disadvantages of this method for research into classroom interaction processes were greatly outweighed by the advantages, I was aware of some serious problems. The key questions of the traditional psychologist when looking at a research technique are: 'Is it reliable and are the results valid?' These are fair questions to ask of the data I have presented so far. Were the observations of John and George given in chapter 3, in order to illustrate the teacher's perceptions of them, a reliable sample of John and George's behaviour? Are my interpretations of the teacher's likely perception of specific behavioural acts valid? I am prepared to argue that the observations were a good and typical sample of the continuous behaviour of the two boys. The observations represent an embarrassingly minute propor-tion of the available observational data on these boys and the choice to include these particular records was made (it seemed as good a reason as any) simply because they were done on the same day. As for their validity it is certain that there are other possible interpretations of the material and the interested reader can work them out for himself. An alternative method might have been to ask the teacher herself to pick out from the observational record the behavioural incidents which she took as support for her constructs. The method I used was meant only to illustrate my case not to prove it. Nevertheless if participant observation is to gain general acceptance as a scientific method it must conform to some rules of procedure and it must be analytic. In practice this means that the observer must (i) know exactly what aspect he is investigating, and (ii) keep systematic notes and indexes. The first dictum is the one that calls for theory.

In chapter 3 I outlined the essentials of Kelly's (1955) personal construct theory. These essentials, that man is continuously and actively engaged in testing out his interpretations of the world which he perceives by means of a repertoire of bi-polar personal constructs, are not hard to grasp. The basic assumption that 'each individual erects for himself a representational model of the world which allows him to make some sense out of it and which enables him to chart a course of behaviour in relation to it' (Bannister and Mair, 1968, p. 6) seems accurate if unremarkable. However, I am yet to be convinced that personal construct theory is as useful as its principal research tool the repertory grid. The grid technique seems to stand very well on its own. This relative neglect of their theory, by researchers who are happy to use their methods, perhaps explains why so many of Kelly's followers give the impression of overselling their theory's importance. Bannister, for example, clearly gets great satisfaction in demonstrating the superiority of Kelly's view of man compared with the narrow visions of the learning theorists, the stimulus response men, and other Ur-behaviourists (this phrase, an appealing one, is from Hudson (1972)). Bannister gives the impression that no other humanistic psychology exists. To read him is to forget that Mead, Sartre, Goffman, Laing, Becker, and others are all fighting the same battle. That's a heterogeneous group of names certainly, but all stand for a social psychology as fundamentally opposed to simple reductionism and as deeply committed to the study of the individual psyche and its relationship to others as Kelly's. Mead's psychology, in particular, seems especially close to personal construct theory. Mead's (1934) symbolic interactionism became especially relevant to me because it is built around the idea of 'expectancies', the very concept that has crept into the empirical minds of educational psychologists. Symbolic interactionism is, perhaps, less of a theory than a way of thinking about collective action. It assumes that man lives in a symbolic as well as a physical environment. These symbols are the guides to action that members of a society follow; the direct guides (norms), the guides to actions we ought to do (ideals) and the subjective guides to individual actions (attitudes). These symbols are meaningful in so far as men are able (most of the time) to predict each other's behaviour and to gauge their own behaviour according to the expectations they believe others to have for them. Mead pointed out that one acts in the perspective supplied by one's relationship with others whose actions reflect roles with which one can identify. To Mead it was by 'taking the role of the other' that we understand the actions of the other. Unhappily, in the hands of Mead's disciples the concept of the role was pushed beyond the bounds of commonsense and Mead's message was lost in an anarchic proliferation of role concepts. None the less, symbolic interactionism is a useful framework for the participant observer. For in order to understand fully the contexts in which events take place their historical development must be known. Garfinkel (1969, pp. 36–7) has written:

> . . . it frequently happens that in order for the investigator to decide what he is looking at he must wait for future developments, only to find that these futures in turn are informed by *their* history and future. By waiting to see what will have happened he learns what it was he previously saw.

This seems to be correct. The first few weeks I spent observing primary school classes baffled me because I could not see how the teachers managed to maintain order. One teacher would call out a child's name and the whole class would be quiet for the next five minutes. Another would stand behind her desk with her hand held up and everyone in the class would quieten as soon as they noticed her. Both teachers were communicating symbolically with the class. These particular symbols meant 'be quiet'. When using them the teacher expects the class to be silent and the pupils have learnt their meanings. The meanings are, in fact, taught in a very traditional way. It took six weeks' observation to discover that the teacher who called out children's names really meant something like: 'John, Freddy, Susan. You are making a noise. If you don't stop I may become cross and belt you.' Eventually I heard her say this and understood what was going on. The teacher who stood behind her desk and raised her hand had taught the children in a similar way that this was her sign meaning that she wanted silence and attention. The theory of learned symbols as guides to action is quite distinct from the empiricist view. The empiricist would maintain that the child belted five weeks before provides the causal link between the teacher's present statement and the pupils' behaviour. An interactionist considers this symbol itself the cause and would argue that methods used to teach the symbols were immaterial. The important point is that a long period of observation is needed in order to recognize the symbols, describe them, and understand how they are learned.

The period I had spent in my initial research school proved extremely valuable. However, since each class was taken by only one teacher I was never able to establish whether the perceptions of individual children by different teachers might vary. It seemed important to know this since if a child was perceived, say, favourably by one teacher and unfavourably by another, it should be possible to determine whether the child's behaviour in the classrooms of the two teachers would differ. From Mead's theory we would certainly expect this to happen.

A research plan was not difficult to formulate. It was decided to observe interactions between teachers and pupils in several primary school classes in different schools. I also thought that in order to investigate the extent to which individual children would be perceived differently by different teachers, it would be interesting to follow through the children from their primary schools to secondary school. To simplify matters a single mixed comprehensive school was chosen together with its five feeder primary schools. The schools were all, of course, in the same local area: a post-war council estate on the outskirts of the city.

Each of the five primary schools was visited for three weeks and most of this time was spent in close observation of the senior class. This stage of the research lasted from October 1970 to March 1971. In April 1971 almost all the children from the five classes I had observed were transferred to the local comprehensive school. It will be useful at this point to note the precise numbers of children involved. This is best shown by Table 5. The table demonstrates that the total number of children in the six classes of the five primary schools studied was 213. It will be seen that at school A two classes were studied. This was because eighteen of the pupils due to transfer from this school to the secondary school were in the class below the senior class. Of these 213 pupils only 177 were transferred to the local comprehensive school. There they were joined by twenty-six children from schools outwith the district bringing the total to 203. At secondary school the pupils were formed into six classes named (in this work) after Scottish castles.

At primary school the following data for each pupil were noted from the school records: (i) Moray House Verbal IQ from a test administered in 1966 when the children were seven years old, (ii) a measure of ability derived from their teachers' grades, and (iii) father's occupation. From a simple questionnaire given by myself the following additional information was obtained: (iv) the number of brothers and sisters they had, and their position in the family, (v) who their friends were in the class.

At secondary school, after transfer, a similar questionnaire was given to provide evidence about changes in the following: (vi) the age at which children wished to leave school, (vii) the job they wished to do, and (viii) who their friends were in class.

At both stages of the research, informal conversations with the children and with the staff were important sources of information. More formally, the repertory grid procedure described in chapter 3 was completed by all the six class teachers at the five primary schools and by four teachers at secondary school. It was impossible in the space of less than one term to observe all the six secondary classes. Since they were unstreamed I chose one class at random. From April to June 1971 I observed almost all the lessons given to 'Edzell' by five teachers. This amounted to twenty-three of the forty-five lesson periods they were given each week. During this

Table 5 *Details of the sample*

Final year primary classes			Number transferred			Secondary classes		
A (i)	Boys	18		Boys	18		Boys	15
	Girls	17		Girls	17	Edzell	Girls	19
	Total	35		Total	35		Total	34
A (ii)	Boys	18		Boys	6		Boys	13
	Girls	16		Girls	12	Corgaff	Girls	21
	Total	34		Total	18		Total	34
B	Boys	17		Boys	17		Boys	15
	Girls	15		Girls	15	Newark	Girls	19
	Total	32		Total	32		Total	34
C	Boys	19		Boys	12		Boys	16
	Girls	19		Girls	18	Kilchurn	Girls	19
	Total	38		Total	30		Total	35
D	Boys	11		Boys	11		Boys	15
	Girls	26		Girls	22	Bothwell	Girls	18
	Total	37		Total	33		Total	33
E	Boys	21		Boys	13		Boys	16
	Girls	16		Girls	16	Doune	Girls	17
	Total	37		Total	29		Total	33
	Boys	104	Other primary schools	Boys	13		Boys	90
	Girls	109		Girls	13		Girls	113
	Total	213		Total	26		Total	203

period individual interviews with each pupil in 'Edzell' were carried out with a view to learning something about his perceptions of himself and others in his class. Finally, for three weeks in November 1971 I revisited the school to obtain data about friendship patterns in 'Edzell' and in other first-year classes.

The periods of classroom observation were used to collect the following data by means of field notes:

(i) A general description of the lesson focusing on the teacher's behaviour. It is often argued by teachers that the first few days with a class are the most important and that they determine the pattern the relationship between the teacher and the pupils will take. For the first three or four lessons each teacher gave I therefore focused on her behaviour.

(ii) Notes on individual children noting all that is done in a given period of time. Thirty minutes was the normal period. This is the sort of record that has been presented so far in chapters three and four.

(iii) Notes on the class as a whole. These were made by scanning the classroom and recording the behaviour of groups and individuals.

(iv) Verbatim notes of teacher and pupil interactions. These notes were made in order that the data could later be analysed in the categories used by Flanders (1970) in his interaction analysis system. This involved noting each instance when the teacher (i) talked about or expressed feelings with the class, (ii) praised the class, (iii) built on the ideas of the pupils, (iv) criticized the pupils, and (v) each instance when the pupils replied to the teacher's questions and (vi) made spontaneous comments.

(v) A diagrammatic representation of the children's seating pattern.

The problem of structuring field notes is one of the principal problems of participant observation. The temptation for the inexperienced worker is to try to note everything. But the result of surrendering to this temptation is not 'everything' but nothing. I stated above that the observer must know what he is looking for and must keep systematic notes and indices. The system that I adopted has now been described. At the completion of the fieldwork phase the notes were cross-indexed.

The details of this may be briefly mentioned. Two main indices were made: (i) a sheet was prepared for each child and every mention of a child in the notes was transferred to the appropriate sheet, and (ii) sheets were prepared for each teacher to which were transferred each occasion the teacher was noted to use modes of interaction which could be categorized by the modified Flanders' analysis system described above.

The second stage of my research was thus about to begin. The idea of following a group of children from primary to secondary school to discover what sorts of adjustment they made and how this was related to their various teachers' perceptions of them, was not, of course, determined by my reading of interaction psychology. However, my belief that procedures and methods should be carefully spelled out certainly follows from the general theoretical perspective I have discussed above. It is interactionist theory which has influenced my perceptions of classroom events and which determines which of those events I shall choose to note down as data.

Chapter 6 From primary to secondary school

The primary school in which I spent my first research year had, as I wrote above, a local reputation for being 'progressive'. It was a pleasant place and I enjoyed being there, but to the extent that I came to think it typical, it misled me. My experience in this school, and much of what I had read, had persuaded me that children transferring from primary to secondary schools would also be moving from 'progressive' to 'traditional' learning contexts. Clearly, my mind has changed on this point and how the change was brought about will be the subject of this chapter. But let me first present some of the evidence that had contributed to my error.

Many writers on education are convinced that the primary school is more 'progressive' than the secondary school. Cave (1968, p. 18) writes: '. . . the secondary schools have much to learn from progressive primary method with its emphasis on the importance of the individual and education through discovery and activity . . .' Cave goes on to warn that there may be some dangers in accepting this suggestion without some understanding of the philosophical and psychological considerations which underlie it. A warning which would have been unnecessary to the new teachers Partridge met who were forced as soon as they entered his secondary school to become (Partridge, 1968, p. 31) 'part of a tradition that has little connection with modern theories and principles of education'. Pedley (1969, p. 121) implies much the same when he writes of curriculum reform in the comprehensive school: 'Hitherto we have relied on the blotting paper memory of most selected children to take in and then, at the appropriate examination, to regurgitate the facts and second-hand thoughts we fed them with.' Blishen came to a similar conclusion from his reading of entries to an *Observer* competition. Children were asked to write about 'The school that I'd like.' Blishen (1969, p. 11) reports:

> For many of them, there was a time when learning was discovery, and teachers seemed to be older partners, and that was in the primary school. There are children's words quoted in this book that glow with the memory of good primary school teaching, when you were fully involved – head, heart, imagination. It is a miserable thing that the step taken by so many of our children, when they pass to the secondary school, should be a step from excitement and acceptance into boredom and rejection.

Such evidence is not in the least conclusive, but it is hard to believe that there is not some truth in it and it had convinced me. However, the three week observation periods I spent in the five primary schools which made up my second sample forced upon me a different conclusion. Some of the discussion that follows may sound critical but any criticism is made not against the schools' failure to meet my standards (whatever they may be), but those of the Scottish Education Department. The SED handbook describes and prescribes the new approach to teaching in the primary school. Its basic philosophy can be seen in this quotation (1965, p. vii):

> The most fundamental changes . . . are those which have arisen from the growing acceptance by teachers of the principles underlying an education based on the needs and interests of the child and the nature of the world in which he is growing up. Through a wide range of experiences the pupil is given opportunities to participate actively in his own learning. As a result, his approach to what is learned is livelier and his final understanding deeper.

There can be no doubt of the reality of the changes that have taken place over the past decade and yet the assumption that most primary school children are taught by activity methods in unstreamed groups, or are busy at individual projects during an integrated day, is only partially true. In practice the infant classes tend to come closer to the SED's ideals than the senior classes where formal methods still tend to be the norm. This gradual movement away from 'progressive' methods as one passes up through the primary school has been noted also by the SED (1965, p. 61):

> For some time now activity methods have been employed to good effect by many teachers of infant classes, but too often from stage PIII [age 8] activity has been replaced by formal methods of instruction which demand little more from the children than compliance with instruction and memorization of facts.

The SED note that teachers begin to adopt more formal techniques from the age of eight. My observations not only confirm this but suggest that by the age of twelve activity methods have been almost wholly abandoned. It seems that the primary school innovations of recent years, non-streaming, activity methods, and the integrated day, have taken firm root amongst the teachers of younger children but are relatively feeble among teachers of senior primary classes. There are several likely reasons for this. First, the teachers of senior primary classes are often older (three of the five studied here were over forty), and it is reasonable to assume that older teachers will have been less influenced by the new methods than their younger colleagues. Second, teachers often wish to prepare their pupils for what they believe are the more formal techniques practised in the secondary school. Finally, the children are older and less easy to control and many teachers find a more formal approach helps their discipline. It will be useful to examine the learning contexts provided by the teachers of these five senior primary classes.

First of all there is no evidence of the group teaching that one might have expected to find in these classes. According to the SED (1965, p. 68): 'The immovable rows of desks which once formed the pattern of seating in primary schools are no longer appropriate.' However, Figure 2 shows that in all but one of the classes the desks were arranged in this way. By seating together children of similar ability one teacher actually managed to teach in streamed rows. In two other schools the seating was also in rows. A third class was taught in streamed groups. School E occupies the most 'progressive' position – unstreamed groups – but more needs to be said about this.

This teacher had ten pupils at tables arranged in a horseshoe so that everybody faced the front. Another twelve sat at tables arranged as forms and these also faced the front. The remaining sixteen sat in five small groups. No streaming was practised because the teacher liked to move pupils around frequently to inhibit the development of friendships of which he disapproved. Its appearance as a class where modern methods are practised is wholly deceptive.

In a detailed examination of the teaching methods practised by the five teachers it was found that only one allocated less than half the timetable to written seatwork. Only two teachers

Figure 2   *Seating arrangements in five senior primary classes*

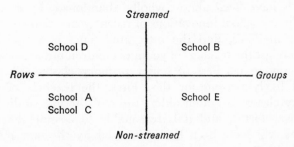

spent more than a token part of the week on projects or on activity work. Table 6 gives the percentages of time spent on five curriculum activities. Written seatwork is not, of course, a curriculum subject; it is descriptive of the way in which many subjects, English, mathematics, and social studies, for example, are commonly taught. It includes compositions and text-book exercises. Activity work includes handicraft and art, as well as activity methods used in other areas of the curriculum. Oral work can occur in any subject, for example, mental arithmetic, discussion or oral comprehension. Kounin (1970) has shown that teachers who provide a greater variety of seatwork activities are more successful in managing their classes than teachers who provide little variety. Kounin's classification of what he terms the pupils' overt behaviour modes is more elaborate than mine but both systems recognize that the way a subject is taught may be more important than what the subject happens to be.

Table 6 *Percentages of week spent in various activities in the senior classes of five primary schools*

School	Written seatwork	Oral work	Activity work	Games	Radio TV
A	37	16	32	9	5
B	55	9	21	11	3
C	54	13	13	7	2
D	50	18	18	13	7
E	64	9	9	5	8

Looking even closer at the face of reality the ideals of the SED seem to fade almost completely. It has already been shown that four of the five classes spent at least half their time in written seatwork. For almost all of this time children were busy at text-book exercises in mathematics or English. The SED (1965, p. 37) state:

... the curriculum is not to be thought of as a number of discrete subjects, each requiring a specific allocation of time each week or month. Indeed, it is quite impossible to treat the subjects of the curriculum in isolation from each other if education is to be meaningful to the child.

However, in none of these classes did I note any attempt by teachers to integrate subjects. Moreover, the SED (1965, pp. 36-7) go on to say:

... as innovations are introduced such aspects of the traditional content as are now seen as unnecessary or irrelevant for the pupils must be pruned. Many of the activities now being recommended in language arts, for example, should occupy time hitherto given to the class reading lesson and to exercises on the technicalities of written English. In arithmetic, lengthy and repetitive mechanical computations should give way to the practical activities and the other aspects of mathematics now being suggested.

My research suggests that, if the sample is a fair one, the majority of children in the senior classes of primary schools are spending up to two thirds of their seatwork time in precisely the sort of work that the SED call 'unnecessary' and 'irrelevant'. This sort of work, for example (Kitto-Jones, 1958, p. 41):

1 Write the following in the PLURAL:
   The fairy's dance; that man; this lady; my baby's cot; it was the woman's shoe.
2 Write out the following and underline the adjectives:
   Under the spreading chestnut tree
   The village smithy stands.
   The smith a mighty man is he,
   With large and sinewy hands.

And this (Anderson, 1961, p. 30):

1 Are you going to w—gh the cake?
2 Joan has a temp—ry job.
3 The plane flew the Atlantic oc—n.
4 The bride walked up the a—le.

Even this has more meaning than the 'writing' exercises some children are made to do. Their books are filled with pages that ook like this:

Cc Cc Cc Cc Cc Cc Cc Cc
Dd Dd Dd Dd Dd Dd Dd Dd
Dad caught a cod.   Dad caught a cod.
Dad caught a cod.   Dad caught a cod.

Some children spent a half-hour every day on this sort of 'writing'. 'Lengthy repetitive mechanical computations' precisely defines most of the arithmetic pupils are required to do. It is still possible to find children working on this sort of sum (and after decimal day, too) (Watson, 1954, p. 113):

12 If 72 bars of soap, each weighing 4 lb., are bought for £14. 8s., what will be gained or lost by selling the soap at 10½d. per pound?
13 A fruiterer bought 6 lb. of grapes for £1. 18s. 8d. If he sells them at 2/10d. per pound find his gain.

Occasionally sums were set with what seems to have been the

aim of baffling as many children as possible. Here is one set by a teacher who disliked giving top marks:

$$\frac{1\frac{5}{16} - \frac{1}{3} \text{ of } \frac{1}{8}}{\frac{1}{2} \text{ of } 1\frac{5}{9} + \frac{1}{4}}$$

Even where activity-related text-books were used it was very unusual for teachers to follow them and they normally instructed the children to pass on to the exercises.

In Table 6 it was shown that in three classes oral work took up around 15 per cent of the timetable. The SED handbook is strongly in favour of this and, after mentioning the need for 'carefully chosen questions' and warning against insisting that children always talk in complete sentences, states (p. 99): 'The teacher's part is primarily to ensure that the atmosphere and seating arrangements of the class are such that opportunities for discussion arise and are taken readily.' Several researchers have paid attention to the sort of questions that teachers and pupils ask and to the characteristics of classroom language. My observations suggest that there are three central reasons – all to do with the teacher rather than the pupil – which detract from useful discussion in the classroom. First, most teachers only ask questions to which they already know the answer. To teachers the answer they want is obvious and it often seems to them that it should be equally obvious to their pupils. Two examples, from many, will illustrate this point. The first comes from a singing lesson; the teacher has noticed a word in the song they are learning and wants to know if the class understand its meaning:

> Teacher holds up the song book. 'There's a word here –
> do you know what it means? We're going back a thousand
> years. A thousand years ago. Just before William the
> Conqueror?' Children look blank. No one seems willing to
> guess. 'Barter. That's what I'm thinking of. A thousand
> years ago people used to barter things instead of using
> money.'
> (School B)

The second example comes from a spelling lesson:

> The class all spell out 'apparatus' in chorus. A bit ragged.
> 'Give me some examples of apparatus.' A boy calls out,

'Kidney machine.' Teacher looks at him. Not very friendly,
I think. The boy repeats his answer. Teacher looks at him
again and appears to consider it. 'No, that's an instrument.'
Class look stunned. 'Oh, come on. There's lots of things.'
(School E)

This tendency of teachers to ask closed-ended questions has
also been noted by Barnes *et al.* (1969) who called them 'pseudo
questions' on the grounds that although they seem open the
way the teacher treats replies – she will accept only one
answer – shows them to be closed-ended. This is one common
difficulty with oral work; everything is so obvious to the
teacher that she rarely troubles to think out alternative
answers either before or after hearing the pupils' replies.

A second difficulty arises from the teacher's assumption
that any answer to her questions must be either wholly correct
or wholly incorrect. It is unusual for a teacher to give or
accept an answer that is simply wrong but a great number of
statements teachers make are only partially true and the idea
that there might be two or more alternative answers never
seems to occur to them. For example, there was a currency in
Anglo-Saxon England and it seems reasonable to regard a
kidney machine as an apparatus. On one occasion I mentioned
to a teacher what I thought an unimportant point that had
occurred in a class discussion. In talking about sports she had
accepted the reply to a question about the origin of the phrase
'boxing ring' that it was so called because the audience sat in
a ring. I had always believed that it was because the 'boxing
ring' used, in fact, to be circular. The teacher was rather
distant about this. 'Well, I don't suppose it matters. They've
probably forgotten by now.' What matters, I suggest, is that
teachers are prepared to accept as correct answers which
strike them as reasonable rather than admit their lack of
knowledge and encourage pupils – if they are interested – to
find out for themselves.

One further difficulty arises in oral work from the teacher's
insistence that only matters she thinks proper are discussed
in the classroom. There is a record in my field notes of a teacher
who wanted the class to write a letter describing the place
where they lived to a child living abroad. The children didn't

think much of their district: 'It's a dump.' 'All tin cans.' 'Nothing to do.' 'A scruffy place.' The teacher warned them about being 'silly' and quickly moved the discussion on to the tourist centres (which few of the children had visited) in the centre of the city. The clearest illustration of this tendency teachers have of moving discussion away from what they feel are sensitive areas occurred during a talk about topics for a debate. The pupils made suggestions and the teacher wrote them on the board after making what she considered suitable alterations. One suggestion was, 'Children should not get the belt':

> 'Oh, how many of you think that children shouldn't get the belt?' Almost all hands go up. 'Well, it looks like you've out-voted yourselves, if you all agree there won't be any debate. I've a feeling that there won't be any debate. I've a feeling that I'm going to veto this one. What does veto mean?' 'Bung it out.' 'Get rid of it.' Several children reply. 'Um, yes. I don't mind but some people . . . now sensible ones.' A girl suggests debating whether they should have a shorter dinner hour and leave school earlier in the afternoon. Teacher likes this suggestion and erases the question about belting and adds this to the list. A few more suggestions come up – going to the moon, capital punishment – a boy suggests, 'Children should be allowed to eat in class.' Lots of calls for this. 'Yes, yes.' 'Oh no,' says the teacher, 'that's silly, we're not having that.' The children are a bit excited at this prospect of having some discussion about their lives in school. 'Children should not be allowed to be teachers' pets' is suggested. There is overwhelming response to this. Lots of enthusiastic agreement. 'Oh, no. Now you are being silly. We're not doing that. Now I want some sensible ones or we'll go back to arithmetic.'
> (School D)

It is not surprising that oral work is so largely unsuccessful. It is frustrated by the teachers' inability to phrase questions adequately, by their failure to accept alternative answers or the possibility of their own error, and by their refusal to allow the children to discuss their own feelings and problems.

I have shown that few of the senior primary classes I
observed spent much time on activity methods. The SED
(1965, p. 61) is keen to stress the importance of these techniques:
'It is vital that teachers should appreciate the need for learning
through activity . . . in all branches of the curriculum and at
all stages.' Some of the teachers in the classes I observed made
their feelings about non-academic activity explicit. One
teacher made no attempt to provide activity projects and even
demonstrated his impatience with the obligatory weekly hour
or so of handwork. The record makes this clear:

> Teacher is pretty sharp with them. 'I think it's a pity you
> made the blue so dark.' The boys look at their painting
> and shrug as the teacher turns away. The boys at the far
> table are not doing any handwork at all. They are thinking
> up names of cars and writing them down. This is a game.
> They go round the table each taking a letter in turn and
> writing down a car name beginning with that letter –
> lamborghini, morris, nash, opel – and so on. The teacher
> ignores them. 'Where did you ever see such a black
> elephant?' he asks a boy who is painting, 'I said shades of
> grey. And you're going to have a hole through that paper.'
> The room is subdued. At one table four boys have a pile of
> Plasticine and a few scraps of cotton-wool. One boy is
> squeezing a lump flat with his ruler. Another pokes a lump
> with his pencil. I ask what they are doing. 'Don't know,'
> they say. 'We started making animals then canoes but they
> didn't work. Do you know what we can make?' Three boys
> take a model – it looks like an inverted pyramid on a
> Plasticine stand – to the teacher. 'What's that supposed to
> be?' he asks. The boys stand around looking defensive
> about it. The teacher says, 'All right, let's have all this stuff
> cleared away, we'll have the girls back soon.'
> (School E)

When they were well practised, however, handicraft and
project lessons could be very successful. At least one teacher
felt that this sort of work helped with her discipline. If children
threatened to become out-of-hand it was always possible for
her to restrict the time they could spend on projects which
they all enjoyed. It is always very difficult to measure whether

or not learning has occurred and yet more difficult to evaluate the efficacy of different styles and methods of teaching. To determine whether modern primary school methods are more successful than traditional methods would be a formidable task. Nevertheless, one's feeling is, and it is shared by the SED's advisors, that the activity and discovery learning of the new primary school are more successful than the alternative of quiet seatwork at formal exercises. More successful in teaching basic school skills *and* that learning can be a satisfying activity.

I have shown that the classes at the senior end of the primary school are organized along 'traditional' and formal lines. The integrated day, the group methods, the activity and discovery work have all virtually disappeared. However, some of these classes were run more formally and more strictly than others. In this respect the classroom regimes did differ to some extent. These differences are worth studying because there is evidence – and it will be mentioned later – that the behaviour of children in their primary school and after they had transferred to secondary school was affected by the way their primary school classroom was organized and controlled.

Table 7 *Percentages of week spent in various activities in a first-year secondary school class*

School	Written seatwork	Oral work	Activity work	Games	Radio TV
Comprehensive	42	13	36	9	0

It is necessary here to examine the nature of the comprehensive school to which the children moved. It was recently formed from a junior and a senior secondary school (in English terms, a secondary modern school and a grammar school) and so exists on two sites a half-mile apart. The old junior secondary, now known as the annexe, houses only the first- and second-year pupils and is wholly unstreamed. The policy of the school is to smooth the transition from primary to secondary as much as possible and with this aim in view the school had begun to introduce just those activity-related methods and integrated subjects that are common in the primary school until the last year or two. It was impossible to study the effects of this teaching systematically since the integrated maths, science, and social studies courses were not introduced until the autumn term after most of the field work had been completed. Table 7 shows the percentages of time spent in different activities.

It is remarkable that the time spent in written seatwork is actually less in the first year of the secondary school than in all but one of the senior classes of the primary schools. Notes made in a class where the new mathematics course was in operation will provide an idea of the atmosphere and of the sorts of learning contexts provided by the three integrated courses:

> The children settle at the four large tables. All the equipment here – shelves, tables, materials – is new. The teacher hasn't said a word yet and is busy with paper work at his desk. Already children are taking the envelopes containing their work modules from the shelves. They talk quite a lot while doing this. Teacher deals with a couple of boys who have approached his desk for help. He hands them their papers which they need for the module. Almost all the children have now begun to work at their desks. The class are fairly quiet now. The boys at the desk nearest me are working from a sheet containing a series of questions like this:
>
> *Complete the following*
>
> . : : 123
>
> : . : 212
>
> : : :
>
> And so on. At another table the children have cut out small squares of paper with the numbers 9, 1, and 6 written on them. The instructions are to:
>
> *Try making different numbers with them, like this*
>
> 9 1 6
>
> 9 6 1
>
> And so on. The sheet has six dotted lines to show the children that there are six possible combinations. The

room is surprisingly quiet though there is a buzz of noise
as children discuss the problems with each other. There
are also people out of their seat as they replace a module
they have finished and take a new one. The teacher
remains seated at his desk and is kept busy aiding children
who approach him.

The sort of learning contexts the children are experiencing
here closely resemble those which they became used to in the
junior classes of their primary schools, and a way of learning
they were thoroughly trained out of in their senior primary
classes – an irony to which we will return.

In one other respect, too, the secondary school teacher
provides greater freedom of action for his pupils than we found
in the primary school. Although in most classrooms desks were
arranged in immobile rows, teachers did not insist that children
always sat in the same seat. Pupils were thus free to sit by
their friends. In mathematics, science, woodwork, art, and
in some social science studies and English lessons it was, in
fact, normal practice for the children to work in groups or
pairs and at tables, not desks. This may seem a small point
but the difference it makes in practice is enormous. Children
taught in groups are able to discuss their work together and
carry out joint co-operative tasks. It enables the teacher to
talk to a group of six or seven children at a time rather than
either to one child or to the whole class. And it makes it
possible for several different parallel sets of work to be continu-
ing at the same time. With the wide diversity of ability in
non-streamed classes it is often essential to do this.

One curious aspect of these findings is that those teachers
who spend so much time and effort tightening up the regime
in the later years of the primary school do so, at least in part,
because they believe that the pupils will be thus better adjusted
to the secondary school. Unknown to each other the primary
and the secondary school are making attempts to meet each
other and over-shooting the mark. The whole stereotyped
notion of the 'progressive' primary school and the 'traditional'
secondary school has been turned on its head. It will be
extraordinary indeed if the children who find the move to
secondary school difficult are those who have been over

socialized for a non-existent situation by their primary school teachers. But there is some evidence that this is happening.

Although the five primary school classes have been discussed together, they did differ in the extent to which they were run on 'traditional' and 'progressive' lines. They also differed (it's not quite the same thing) in the degree of control they exercised over their pupils. Though there has been little research in this area, many educationists, for example, Berg (1969) and Neill (1968), are entirely convinced that schools which allow considerable autonomy to their pupils thus provide more effective and satisfactory learning contexts than

Figure 3   *Conditions of access to classrooms outside lesson times*

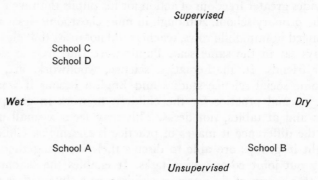

do schools which place many restrictions on pupils. It seemed interesting to look at the five primary schools in this respect. One good example which shows how considerably the degree of institutional control practised by the five schools varied, is afforded by the conditions under which children were allowed access to classrooms outside lesson times. Figure 3 will clarify the argument.

School E did not permit access to the classrooms at these times under any conditions and thus operates the strongest system. Among the access-permitted group the strongest position is represented by the top left-hand box where pupils are allowed in the classrooms at these times only on rainy days and then only under supervision. This is the practice at schools C and D. The weakest position is represented by the bottom right-hand box where pupils are given access to classrooms even on dry days and without supervision. Only school B allows pupils this much freedom. School A occupies a mid-position and allows access only on wet days but without supervision.

This is a good example because it shows very clearly the different levels of control that schools can adopt. To measure this attribute a 'scale of control' was constructed. There are two separate aspects to consider, (i) the school outside the classroom, and (ii) within the classroom. These must be kept distinct because the school outside the classroom is governed by all the teachers whereas the classroom is governed by one teacher only. It would be quite possible to find a school where order was strongly maintained without the classroom but weakly maintained within some individual classrooms; in fact, this is a fairly common situation. Six items were designed to measure the degree of control in the school outside the classroom. Among them are: *Are there separate playgrounds for boys and girls?* and, *Are pupils lined up and supervised on entry to school?* It is possible to argue that schools which separate children by sex at break and which line them up in rows before they may enter or leave school are operating a stronger system of control than those which do not bring these areas of pupil behaviour under the rules of the school. Six items were designed to measure the degree of control practised in the classroom. Among them are: *Are pupils allowed to choose their own seats?* and, *Are there class monitors?* The completed scale was thus composed of twelve items. The scale resembles those discussed by Lambert, Bullock and Millham (1970) in their handbook for the sociological investigation of the school. The full list of items is given in Appendix A. Each item was treated as a four-point scale. For example, on the item, *What are the conditions of access to classrooms outside lesson times?* which was mentioned above, school E, which did not permit such access at all, was given a score of 4, schools C and D received scores of 3, school A a score of 2, and school B a score of 1. The schools which received the lowest scores are held to operate a relatively lax degree of control and those with higher scores are held to operate a relatively firm degree of control. The lowest possible score is 12, and the highest possible score 48. It is possible to relate the scores to aspects of the children's behaviour after their transfer to secondary school.

The scores of the five primary schools, their senior classes, and those of the secondary school are shown in Table 8.

These data show that, compared with the secondary school, the primary schools all operate fairly weak control over pupils outside the classroom. In some primary schools the classrooms are run as liberally as the rest of the school. This is the case in schools A, B and (marginally) C. However, the senior classes in schools D and E are particularly rule-bound. This suggests that practice in these classrooms has got out of step with the general ethos of their schools. Their regimes are also very different from those of the secondary school classrooms.

What happens when children from these classes transfer from the strongly disciplined 'traditional' classrooms they have been accustomed to for several years, to the relatively weakly

Table 8   *Scores on a scale of institutional control*

School	A	B	C	D	E	Sec.
Outside class	8	11	14	10	14	20
Classroom	10	13	17	24	22	12
Total	18	24	31	34	36	32

disciplined and almost 'progressive' first-year secondary school classes? Lacking the strict control they have been used to one would expect them to be unsettled and to become unruly and difficult to handle in the classroom. It was possible to test this hypothesis.

At the end of these children's first term at secondary school they were assessed by their teachers on two measures, (i) effort, and, (ii) behaviour. From these assessments it was possible to determine whether the low scores would be allocated randomly among the pupils from all five primary schools or whether pupils from schools D and E would be over-represented. This hypothesis was partially confirmed. The scores for the girls *were* randomly distributed. In fact, very few girls were assessed as lacking effort or being poorly behaved. Among the boys, however, it was found that those from schools D and E were over-represented among the low scorers. Of the twenty-four boys from these two schools fully eighteen were assessed as being below the median in these respects. This difference is significant at the o·o1 level.

The lower secondary school has been shown to have a more relaxed degree of classroom control than primary schools D and E. Pupils from these schools were used to very different conditions. It is ironic that teachers gave as one reason for their relative strictness the story that they were preparing their pupils for secondary school. When these pupils arrive at the secondary school they perceive the less rigorous control there as a sign of 'softness' and exploit this unaccustomed freedom by misbehaving in a way they were firmly prevented from doing in their primary schools. It seems that both primary and secondary school are basing decisions about their curriculum and teaching organization on misconceptions about each other. The primary teachers believe that the secondary school operates a very formal and strict regime and accordingly begin to prepare their pupils for this while the secondary school, believing that the primary schools have accustomed their pupils to 'progressive' methods, make special efforts to design a suitable curriculum for their needs.

There has been relatively little investigation of the difficulties experienced by children on transfer from primary to secondary school. Nisbet and Entwhistle (1969) have shown that children from poorer backgrounds are most adversely affected. However, most research has been somewhat unproductive. The reasons for this may lie in the lack of direct observation and paucity of theoretical analysis. A methodology restricted to the examination of gains or losses in IQ after transfer to secondary school cannot explain why these changes should occur. In this chapter I have tried to describe actual practice in five senior primary classes. I have shown that this bears little resemblance to the recommendations of the SED. And, perhaps more surprisingly, little resemblance either to the integrated teaching methods newly introduced into the secondary school. This detailed approach leads me to make three substantive conclusions: (i) at the point of transition the contexts of learning provided by primary and secondary schools seem not to be significantly different, (ii) secondary schools which reorganize their teaching methods on the assumption that incoming pupils will be used to 'progressive' methods may be acting under a misconception, and (iii) the children who seem to experience most difficulties in moving from one type of school to another are boys going from a strictly governed classroom to a relatively freer one.

Chapter 7 Pupil behaviour and teacher perception in secondary school

In chapter 3 the repertory grid procedure was described and the common constructs of the eight teachers studied in my first research school were examined. In chapter 5, outlining the second stage of the research, I mentioned that three secondary school teachers completed this repertory grid. Three is a much smaller number than I would have ideally liked. The problem was to allow sufficient time for the teachers to get to know the class. I felt that in one term anything less than three periods a week would not be enough. 'Edzell', the class primarily studied at this stage, was taught by more than a dozen teachers, but only five of these faced the whole class for more than three periods a week. One of these teachers effectively prevented me from observing her classes (the only one that did), and another felt unable to complete the repertory grid since even after three lessons a week for twelve weeks she felt that she still did not know the class sufficiently well. The sample of secondary teachers was thus reduced to three.

In this chapter the common constructs which these teachers used in their perceptions of the pupils in 'Edzell' will be examined. Clearly we can expect that some pupils will be favourably or unfavourably perceived by all teachers. About other children, however, we can expect them to be in disagreement. The hypothesis is that the behaviour of children in classes where they are perceived unfavourably by the teacher, will be different from their behaviour in classes where they are perceived favourably.

The complete list of constructs elicited from the three secondary teachers is given in Appendix B. One of the disadvantages of the repertory grid procedure is that in allowing for personal constructs one makes comparisons between the systems of different individuals extremely difficult. It is possible, however, to pick out some common constructs. Only three constructs are shared by all three teachers; they are:

Bright – Dull
Lively – Lumpish
Likeable – Less likeable

Two other constructs are shared by two of the three teachers:

Well behaved – Less well behaved
Sociable – Less sociable

In order to determine the extent of the agreement between the three teachers' perceptions of the class the construct rank was calculated for each pupil in 'Edzell' on each of the three teachers' grids. For each pupil there were thus three different construct ranks. The ranks were, in fact, calculated separately for boys and girls. Sometimes teachers perceived girls so much more favourably than boys that a boy might have construct rank 10, and yet, since the first nine ranks are given to girls, be the most favourably perceived boy in the class. The extent of agreement between three or more sets of ranks is calculated by the coefficient of concordance. Concordances for these sets of construct ranks were:

Boys $W = 0.67$ N. 15
Girls $W = 0.53$ N. 20

Both figures are significant beyond the 0.05 level. There is enough agreement here to show that the teachers are talking about the same thing but it is clear that they are by no means in total agreement. It is my intention to explore the details of this agreement and disagreement.

In order to make comparisons the fifteen boys in this class were divided into three groups: (i) ranks 1–5 favourably perceived, (ii) ranks 6–10 mid-group, and (iii) ranks 7–15 unfavourably perceived. There were twenty girls and they were also divided into three groups: (i) ranks 1–7 favourably perceived, (ii) ranks 8–13 mid-group, and (iii) ranks 14–20 unfavourably perceived. An example will make the matter clear. If a child has the following construct ranks 1, 5 and 3, we can see that the teachers all agree that he is favourably perceived. Total agreement like this was relatively uncommon. All teachers were agreed in perceiving four children favourably and another four unfavourably. One child was agreed to fall in the mid-group. The three teachers were more or less agreed about seven children who were perceived to be either favourably perceived or as being in the mid-group. There was a similar level of agreement about eleven children who were either seen as coming in the mid-group or perceived unfavourably. The remaining seven children were the subject of disagreement to the extent that one (or two) teachers perceived them favourably and two (or one) perceived them unfavourably. One girl had to be excluded from the analysis since she was absent so often that only one teacher could remember who she was when it came to completing the repertory grid. This girl left at the end of the term so her exclusion is of little importance.

It has been my contention throughout this work that only close observation of classroom processes can reveal the importance of teachers' perceptions upon pupil behaviour. In order to investigate this relationship I shall examine, in case study form, the observed classroom behaviour of four children. Alec A, who will be discussed first, is favourably perceived by each of the four teachers concerned, Ian H is agreed to be unfavourably perceived, and Helen H and Ronald B fall into the small but interesting category of children about whom teachers have widely divergent perceptions.

In chapter 5 some different types of observations made in this study were described. Here types (ii) notes on individuals over a sustained period, (iii) classroom scanning, and (v) verbatim notes on teacher/pupil interaction, were all used. The following classes were observed:

English	Mrs A	10 lessons
English	Mrs C	12 lessons
Maths	Mr D	14 lessons
Science	Mrs E	14 lessons

Finally, in the reports I have drawn on data obtained during interviews with the pupils.

Case 1 Alec A

Primary school: D
IQ: 91
Primary class position: 2nd
Family size: 3/youngest

Born: January 1959
Father: Foreman
Wants to leave at 18
Member of favourably perceived friendship clique at primary and secondary school.

Alec is an interesting boy. He is far brighter than the IQ of 91 would seem to indicate. All teachers agree that he is *very bright* and *very lively*. His behaviour is not seen as particularly good, Mrs C and Mrs A are agreed that he merely tends to be *well behaved*. Mr D thinks he is *very pleasant*, to Mrs C he is *attractive*, and to Mrs A *sensible*. Mrs C finds him *very sociable* and Mrs C and Mrs A agree that he is *friendly* and *outgoing*. Alec's primary teacher seems to concur with this view, she says he is *very alert, very bright* and *very knowledgeable*. However, she is even less pleased with his behaviour than his secondary teachers and says he tends to be *poorly behaved*.

There are many references in the field notes to Alec's academic style. The following extracts will illustrate what I consider some essential points. Field notes are identified by the name of the teacher and a number indicating the particular lesson observed.

> *Mr D 9* 'Who can see this sequence?' Lots of people look puzzled. Alec puts his hand up. 'Alec,' says the teacher. The sequence is: 1 1; 2 2; 3 6; 4 24; 5 120. Alex works it out aloud. 'One times one is one, one times two is two, two times three is six, four times six is twenty-four and five times twenty-four is one hundred and twenty. Then the next one must be six times one hundred and twenty. You could also do it by saying one times two times three and so on 'till you got to six and that would be the same answer. It's – er – seven hundred and twenty.' Teacher says this is right and starts to explain it on the board.
> *Mrs C 4* 'Alec, you can find out what part of the Bible the Apocalypse is in for homework on Wednesday seeing

as you're always going on about homework.' 'It's in Revelations, Miss.' 'I want you to tell me on Wednesday, not now.'

Mrs A 5 Teacher writes,
          PRSVRYPRFCTMNKPYTHSPRCPTSTN
on the board. She tells the class that one letter is missing. 'What is the missing letter and what does it say?' This is supposed to be a game but everybody looks awfully puzzled and anxious. Alec calls, 'E, it's got to be E.' He works it out apart from the word 'precepts' which he does not know.

Mrs E 2 Teacher writes on the board, 'The apparatus was used as in the drawing. When we first heated the outside of the beaker . . . We then saw small bubbles of . . . rising slowly to the surface of the water (etc.).' The children are supposed to fill in the blanks. 'Do we have to write exactly that?' asks Alec. 'Well you've got your own notes on the experiment and they may not be in the same order. But for most people I think they'd better stick closely to that.'

There is evidence here that Alec is not only bright but bright in all his lessons. His ability to grasp mathematical points was impressive. In his English lessons with Mrs C we have an indication of his eagerness in discussion work. Mrs C has obviously picked up his demands for homework, too. His approach to the string of consonants given by Mrs A is also noteworthy. Most of the class never seriously attempted it. When told that one letter was missing the class started to guess wildly. Alec knew not only that the letter must be a vowel but chose the correct one. In the event he still couldn't work it all out but there was nothing wrong with his strategy. The note from his science lesson is almost unique. Alec clearly thought it boring to have to copy from the blackboard and add the missing words. Here he effectively (effectually too) challenged the legitimacy of the teacher's role. The teacher's disciplinary role is often challenged but she is usually master over the curriculum. These extracts fairly completely demonstrate both the style Alec adopts in the classroom and the range of his ability. There are as many notes concerning his tendency to misbehave. A few representative extracts are presented here.

Mr D 2 Teacher is helping Douglas. Alec pummels the desk and leans back on his chair. He talks to William and Stuart who are turning around and grinning. Alec pretends to fall asleep on his desk. Tom, sitting next to him, pulls his ear lifting Alec's head up and dropping it down again. They play this game several times. Alec sits up at last and talks to William.

Mrs C 3 Class are clearing up coloured pencils after sketching in their books. Alec and William are laughing together. – Alec and William getting much more noisy now. Alec starts to draw the curtains to and fro. He is not doing any work. Finished early I suppose.

Mrs A 7 Class are writing a composition. – Alec and William giggle to themselves. Teacher walks over to them and tells them to move apart. – Noise grows. – Alec and William move together again. They chatter loudly as the teacher calls the register. – Lots of fuss and noise. Teacher threatens class with dictation if they are not quiet. Alec sings, 'Dic – dic – tation corp-oration.' Teacher misses this. He starts to pull faces. 'Alec, stop that. Alec, now we'll have no more of that,' orders the teacher. He starts writing again.

Alec's teachers also perceive him as *sociable* and *likeable*. That he readily interacts with other children is clear from the extracts. As for his being likeable I can only say that this was how he was perceived. These extracts will suffice to illustrate that Alec could often be badly behaved. In Mr D's class he would usually chatter with his friend William when he had finished his work. For some reason Mr D rarely bothered about this. Mrs C was stricter and it is interesting that when she tells Alec and William to stop talking they stop – for a while at least. In Mrs A's class Alec could be, and often was, very noisy and cheeky. He wouldn't have dared to chant mocking rhymes in, for example, Mrs C's or Mrs E's class. When I asked him about all the noise he made he said he only started talking when he was bored. About French lessons, for example, where he was terribly noisy he said, 'Ah, I don't like French. I'm just not interested in it.' And there we have it. The point about Alec is that his sheer ability and obvious enthusiasm when his interest was sparked were sufficient to weight his teachers' perceptions heavily in his favour. They are not unaware of his tendency to disrupt things when he feels bored but there are signs that they don't blame him for it.

My assessment of Alec's situation suggests that he knows that he is bright, knows that his teachers know he is bright and knows also that they know that he knows they know he is bright. We can assume that his teachers have a parallel degree of knowledge and meta-knowledge. Alec's awareness of his teacher's knowledge and meta-knowledge enables him to negotiate successfully with them the behavioural concomitants of his identity as 'bright'. For example, when he asks his science teacher if he can write up the account of an experiment the class have just performed in his own words, rather than copy from the board, it is certain that he knows that the teacher will allow him to do this. And she does. But it is clear from her reply that she is making an exception for Alec. 'Most people,' she says, 'had better stick pretty closely to what's on the board.' Alec is here transacting with the teacher an important aspect of his self-identity. The teacher implicitly recognizes his own evaluation of himself as 'bright'. In a similar way Alec manages to transact with most of his teachers licence to pursue his own activities (often potentially disruptive) when he has finished his work.

Case 2   Ian H

Primary school: A	Born: April 1959
IQ: Unknown	Father: Decorator
Primary class position: 15th	Wants to leave at 16
Family size: 3/youngest	Member of poorly perceived friendship cliques in primary and secondary school.

With the exception of Mrs C who sees Ian as tending to be *bright*, he is generally seen as tending to be *dull*. There is agreement that he is not *lively*. Mrs A perceives him as *stolid* and Mr D regards him as tending to have a *weak personality*.

Mrs C seems to be giving him the benefit of doubt and says he tends to be *lively*. All are agreed that he tends to be *misbehaved*. Mrs A finds him *silly*, Mrs C says he is *less attractive*, only Mr B finds him *pleasant*. Mrs C says he is *sociable*, Mrs A *retiring*, and Mrs D tending to be *sociable*. His primary teacher seemed to agree. She saw him as *talkative* and tending to be *lazy* and *shy*, but also tending to be *bright* and *interested*. There are references in the field notes which will illustrate Ian's classroom style.

> *Mrs C 5*　Ian reads a passage from the book. Teacher picks him up on his pronunciation. He elides the 't' sound in 'bottom'. He isn't very happy at being corrected. He repeats it but the second attempt is no better than the first.
> *Mrs A 1*　Ian reads his composition. He has written about two lines. Everybody laughs at him. The cover is falling off his exercise book. It is very untidy.
> *Mrs E 9*　Ian, George, Angus and Ronald are still fiddling with the Plasticine. (They have been making plaster moulds of leaves.) They have messed up their moulds and the plaster has gone hard. Now they have nothing to do. Ian looks particularly lost. He is just standing there doing nothing.

There is no evidence that Ian shows any special ability in any of his classes. There are several signs that his written English is poor and although his reading doesn't appear to be below average one teacher, at least, commonly corrects his speech. In science we see him in a typical position, with a group of poorly achieving boys who have no work to do because they have not been able to cope with the task they have been given. It is not surprising that he is generally perceived as *dull* rather than *bright*. His behaviour in different classes has a similar unity.

> *Mrs C 3*　Teacher talks to Ian. Evidently he was sent out of the room this morning for kicking his feet about. He is getting a good warning now, too.
> *Mrs A 5*　Ian and Kathleen are throwing their pumps at each other. Ian leaves his seat and walks over to Kathleen. Teacher is with Ronald looking at his book. She turns round. Ian goes back to his place.

Mrs E 11 Nobody is very keen to stop working with the microscopes. There is a bit of noise. 'Everybody look here,' calls the teacher. 'Ian, Bruce, George.' These three are wrestling with each other's arms on the bench top.

One curious point about Ian's classroom behaviour is that these incidents of chattering and minor horseplay with Kathleen and then Bruce and George were comparatively rare. Ian was nowhere near as badly behaved as Alec and yet he was perceived as being the worse behaved of the two. There was general agreement that Ian was not particularly sociable. This can be borne out to some extent by my observation that for the first three weeks of the term he sat with the girls rather than with the boys. Eventually he got to know Bruce, Angus, and Douglas and he often sat near them. I was not able to talk to Ian very readily. He seemed to me to be a little uneasy and suspicious. I did eventually get to know him and discovered that he had considerable antipathy towards some of his teachers. The following conversation will illustrate this:

RN   How's it going with Mrs A these days?
IH   I dunna like her much. She tends to be the same as the other teachers. But I think she should be stricter. Hazel K goes too far.
RN   Yes, what about French?
IH   Oh, if everyone in the class is making a noise – well, she'll look at me and she'll give me the blame while everyone else is doing it, too.
RN   Um, I saw you with Mrs H yesterday. What's she got against you?
IH   Well, she's the same as Mrs T, ken, if – I always sit at the back when I go in the room and she puts me in a special seat and I hate it and I didn't – Sometimes I shift up a bit and she tells me to sit there while everybody else – I think the other boys are making as much noise and all that as me and she just puts me there every week.

In fact, Ian appeared to me to be fundamentally quiet. In Mr D's classes I have no notes on him whatever which means he must have neither answered questions nor misbehaved in any noticeable way. He liked Mr D and disliked those teachers who, in his view, allow him to misbehave. He regards it as the teacher's job to keep the class and himself in order and so if he is led to misbehave it is they who are failing in their job. This is perhaps one clue to explain why Mr D finds him *pleasant* and Mrs A *silly*. Ian knows that he is not highly thought of by his teachers and he knows that he is not good at school work. In the same way his teachers know what he thinks of them. His identity in the classroom has been managed by his teachers and has been transmitted by them to the class and to Ian himself. He has been unable to negotiate a more favourable self-identity. Ian had come to expect that teachers were not going to like him and had resigned himself to the inevitable. He certainly felt 'picked on' and probably not without reason. To this extent he seems to be resisting the teachers' power to control his identity. Unfortunately, this resistance is seen by the teachers as 'sullenness' and simply serves to reinforce their perceptions.

Teachers' perceptions of Alec and Ian agreed. Alec was favourably perceived and Ian unfavourably perceived by them all. The two following cases consider a boy and a girl about whom teachers disagreed.

Case 3   Helen

Primary school: E	Born: October 1958
IQ: 103	Father: Joiner
Primary class position: 17th	Wants to leave at 18
Family size: 5/youngest	Member of poorly perceived friendship clique at primary school and favourably perceived clique at secondary school.

Helen was perceived differently by each of the three teachers considered here. Mrs C saw her favourably, Mr D placed her in the mid-group and Mrs A saw her unfavourably. Mrs C says she is *bright*, Mrs A and Mr D that she is *less bright*. Mrs C says she is *lively*, Mrs A says she tends to be *stolid*, and Mr D finds she has a *weaker personality*. Mrs C considers Helen to be *well behaved* and Mrs A says she tends to be *silly*, though Mr D says she is *very pleasant*. All agree that she is *sociable*. The observations of Helen's classroom behaviour may be helpful in understanding this variance in her teachers' perceptions of her.

Mr D 9 Class are working out the number of different ways to arrange the days of the week. Helen and Eileen are comparing notes. Helen puzzles out the next problem, how many ways the letters ABCD can be arranged. She gets this right without any trouble.
Mrs C 6 Helen reads. She reads very clearly. Everyone seems to understand.

There is little to say of Helen's academic behaviour. The notes are rather sparse. We can deduce from this that she wasn't keen on answering questions or joining in discussion. There are more observations on her behaviour.

Mrs C 3 Helen is with Irene and William – they are making a lot of noise. John, Roderick and Alec are also chattering with them. Teacher asks, 'How many of you have finished? I'll give you two more minutes to finish your pictures. Meanwhile will you work quietly? Quietly!' Helen, Alec and William are talking again. 'All right then, please, I'll collect in these pencils. Hurry up. Can I have all these pencils please?' They pack up. Helen is still fooling about with William and treading on his toes.
Mrs A 4 Helen is talking to Judy. They are writing notes and passing them along to Eliza and Margaret. – Helen gets out of her seat. She makes a great stamping noise with her feet on the floor. – Helen still clattering her feet on the bench. Teacher tells her not to fidget. At this a rash of fidgeting breaks out from the girls at this corner. Teacher reads on with the story for a minute or two. 'Stop fidgeting will you.' She is getting cross.

These are interesting data. Helen was perceived as *well behaved* by Mrs C and as tending to be a *nuisance* by Mrs A. Sure enough there is only one note of Helen's chattering in Mrs C's class and there is no certainty that Mrs C noticed Helen specially – she was with a large group of others – but in Mrs A's classes we see Helen becoming more and more rowdy. Not only talking to her friends when she was meant to be writing, but stamping her feet, giggling, and eating sweets. To Mrs C Helen is *bright* and *lively*, to Mrs A she tends to be *less bright* and *stolid*. The field notes suggest that there is some objective basis for these discrepant perceptions. Whether or not Helen's behaviour in the classes of the two English teachers was directly influenced by their perceptions of her is not a question that can yet be answered.

When I talked to Helen she said that she liked Mrs C and Mr D but not Mrs A. She thought Mrs C and Mr D were 'good' teachers, and she was able to elaborate a little:

HH   Well, the good teachers they don't always moan at you. They're strict but they're good teachers.

RN   What about bad teachers?

HH   Well, always complaining at you and that – always telling you to be quiet. Won't let you talk quietly – so long as you don't make a lot of noise. – Like Mrs A is a bit soft – she doesn't warn us properly. She lets us get away with shouting and everything.

This was a very common response. Most children really did seem to hold the teacher responsible for the noise and disruption they made. At her primary school Helen was something of a nonentity. Her primary teacher seems to have found her generally unremarkable. On moving to secondary school she has made friends with a different (and more favourably perceived) group of girls and has found that she is good at some subjects, for example, maths. In Mr D's class she finds herself able to do the work and, in this relatively well disciplined class, does well. In Mrs C's class, also well disciplined, her behaviour follows the same pattern. However, Mrs A finds the class more difficult to control, and Helen, who has very definite ideas about how teachers should behave, reacts to this relatively loose control by mischievousness with her friends. A form of misbehaviour which is clearly meant to tease the teacher.

Case 4 Ronald

Primary school: C
IQ: 84
Primary class position: 20th
Family size: 5/third

Born: January 1959
Father: Joiner
Wants to leave at 15
Member of poorly perceived friendship clique at primary and secondary school.

Whereas Helen was unfavourably perceived by Mrs A but favourably by Mrs C, and moderately by Mr D, Ronald is seen favourably by Mrs C and Mrs A, but unfavourably by Mr D. To Mrs C and Mrs A he is tending to be *bright, lively,* and *imaginative* but to Mr D he was tending to be *less able, easily led, immature* and with a *weak personality.* Mr D also thinks Ronald tends to be *less sociable* while Mrs C and Mrs A find him *sociable* and *outgoing.* Mr D agrees to the extent that he finds him *pleasant*, and Mrs C and Mrs A find him *likeable* and tending to be *sensible.* The field note extracts will illustrate his adaptation to the classrooms of his several teachers.

Mr D 7 Teacher gives out instructions about the work. Ronald chews his pencil. He seems to be listening. – Seems like Ronald has stopped work now. He is reading the wall posters about the Vikings and rocking on his chair. – It turns out that Ronald who has done nothing for fifteen minutes is stuck on the sixth of thirty-six sums.

Mrs C 6 Ronald sits by the window. Teacher reads the story. Ronald looks as he always does, very quiet.

Mrs A 2 Teacher is reading a poem. Ronald rocks on his seat. There is some noise in the class. Hazel is sent out of the room for misbehaviour. Ronald looks at the book. He is still rocking on his chair. He looks bored and pokes his teeth with his pen. – A great noise in the room now. Irene leans forward and tries to talk to Ronald. He is just idly kicking the chair and not taking much notice of all the row that is going on. Irene pushes his bag off the back of his chair and on to the floor. Ronald makes no protest and simply picks it up while still chewing his pen.

I find Ronald's behaviour remarkably stable right across his lessons. It is possible that he is favourably perceived by

Mrs A because he doesn't ever misbehave even when everyone around him is. The forbearance he shows when Fay, Bruce, and Irene all at different times try to pull him into their messing about is extraordinary. Mrs C also seems to appreciate his stability in this respect. Mr D, however, is more interested in his academic behaviour. That he will sit for a quarter of an hour having done only six sums is a mark against him so far as Mr D is concerned. He doesn't answer questions and he doesn't do much work. But he is remarkably quiet and undisturbed by commotion.

It is interesting to learn that Ronald says he gets on quite well with Mrs C and with Mrs A, but not with Mr D. When he is talking about the teachers he never mentions their discipline; presumably it doesn't affect him. The subject matter seems to be what interests him or not. In conversation he said:

RN How do you get on in Mr D's lessons?

RB Well, sometimes I have difficulty in adding and subtracting.

RN And English?

RB Well, Mrs C gives us more stories and she makes us write a lot. And reading stories. You learn things – well, about plants, science fiction and that.

Ronald's stable pattern of behaviour has clearly been built up in his primary school where his teacher thought well of him. It is interesting that one of his secondary teachers finds this adjustment unsatisfactory. It is not clear yet whether Ronald is aware that Mr D has a poor opinion of him, and it is not clear either whether he will be able to modify his behaviour in a way that will be favourably seen by Mr D.

In this chapter I have described the behaviour of four children; Alec, who is favourably perceived by all three teachers, Ian, who is perceived unfavourably by all his teachers, and Helen and Ronald, who are perceived favourably by some teachers and unfavourably by others. I have related the teachers' perceptions of these children to the children's behaviour in their classes. It seems suggestive that the two pupils about whom there was disagreement say they got on well with the teachers who, it turns out, perceived them favourably, and say they do not get on well with those who perceive them unfavourably. We have seen also that there are often noticeable differences in their academic and other behaviour depending upon whether the teacher liked them or not. I have suggested that an interactionist perspective can help to make this process understandable. The teacher's expectations for the pupil will affect his academic behaviour in so far as his teacher's interactions with him contribute to this self-concept. Ian's self-identity does seem dependent on the teachers' view of him, but possibly Ronald's self-concept is less open to influence from his teachers. Ian knows that he is not highly thought of by his teachers and seems to have internalized their view of him. Ronald, however, seems to be unaware that Mr D sees him unfavourably and his self-concept is possibly less affected.

Chapter 8 The perception of pupils by primary and secondary teachers

In the last chapter I discussed the extent to which secondary teachers shared perceptions of their pupils. On the whole it was found that they did substantially agree. In this chapter the primary school teachers' perceptions will be compared with those of the secondary teachers. We can expect that in some cases the perceptions of teachers from both schools will be similar. In other cases we can expect to find disagreement.

There were some difficulties in making these comparisons. First, as I have shown, the repertory grid makes direct comparison between the construct systems of one teacher and those of another rather difficult. In the previous chapter I demonstrated that the common constructs of the secondary teachers were: *Bright – dull, Well behaved – poorly behaved, Lively – stolid, Likeable – less likeable,* and *Sociable – unsociable.* The six primary teachers also tended to use these constructs. A procedure was developed for establishing the degree of congruence between a pupil's primary teacher's view of him and his secondary teacher's view. The construct rank measure has already been explained. It gives an indication of how favourably a pupil is perceived in relation to his classmates. The pupil's construct ranks derived from the data given by their primary teachers were compared with the construct rank derived by averaging the construct ranks given by each of the secondary teachers.

The agreement between these measures seemed considerable. In this case there is no really appropriate statistic for measuring the degree of congruence but for no fewer than twenty-three of the children in 'Edzell' there were less than seven points of difference between the two sets of ranks. That is to say most pupils are seen more or less similarly by their primary teachers and secondary teachers. For ten children the difference was greater than this. They may be divided into two groups: (i) those who are perceived much more favourably by their secondary teachers than by their primary teachers, and (ii) those who are perceived much more favourably by their primary teachers than by their secondary teachers. Four children fell into the former group and six in the latter group.

Inspection of the available data has revealed no statistically significant reason why teachers in the two schools should have such discrepant perceptions of these particular children. Nevertheless, there is some tentative evidence that a few children were in some ways disturbed by the transfer and that this was reflected in their behaviour. In the following case study the classroom style of one girl will be analysed to show how her behaviour altered as she moved from primary to secondary school.

Case 5 Kathleen

Primary school: A(i)   Born: January 1959
IQ: 92   Father: Labourer
Primary class position: 10th Wants to leave at 15
Family size: 4/eldest   Member of favourably per-
                         ceived friendship cliques at
                         primary and secondary schools.

Kathleen is perceived more favourably by her primary teacher than by her secondary teachers. At secondary school Mrs C and Mrs A agree in seeing her moderately favourably and say she tends to be *bright* and tends to be *well behaved*. Mr D, however, finds her *dull*. This rather mediocre assessment is in marked contrast to the view Kathleen's primary teacher had of her. According to the teacher she is *bright, quiet, forthcoming*, and *confident*. The following notes were made of Kathleen in her primary class.

Primary A(i)   Kathleen is sitting in her chair taking her plimsolls out of her bag. Games lesson is in fifteen minutes. She puts on her plimsolls. Teacher gives out the SRA books for children who have correction to do. Kathleen takes her time over changing her shoes. She leaves her seat and takes a card from the teacher's desk. She sits down and begins her work. She talks to her neighbour occasionally. There is a fair bit of noise in the class. Kathleen talks to a boy who passes her desk. She ticks off the responses in her SRA book. Seems to be paying attention now. There is quite a lot of noise but she writes all the time. Eventually, after a few minutes, she gets up again to take a new card from the box. She sorts through the box looking around the room. She puts the lid on the box and then goes to the teacher's desk and sorts through the papers there for a workcard. She finds one and takes it to the box. There she finds several other pupils and they talk for a couple of minutes. The others leave having got their workcards and Kathleen begins to sort through the box again. It is clear now that she is tidying it up. She continues with this task working steadily while the teacher reads to the class a story someone has written. It is good and everyone listens. Only Kathleen and a couple of others are out of their seats now. It is Susan's story. She is smiling and looking a bit sheepish but obviously pleased. Teacher praises her. Kathleen is working at the box quietly and steadily. It is nearly time for games.

These data are sufficient to demonstrate the nature of Kathleen's adaptation to the particular classroom context she found herself in. The class is particularly noisy because the lesson period is coming to an end and most of the pupils have finished their work. Kathleen, too, has completed the bulk of her work for the morning and in the notes she is observed to complete her corrections without being greatly distracted by the noise and movement around her. It is most interesting to see how she usefully fills in the last five minutes before games by tidying the SRA box. This is not a job the teacher has asked her to do. Kathleen is no more responsible for the box's tidiness than anybody else. It is reasonable to suppose that the teacher appreciated this helpful initiative and it is perhaps not surprising that she should perceive Kathleen as *forthcoming* and *confident*. It is possible that the relatively unstructured nature of this particular classroom provided Kathleen with just the sort of climate that was most appropriate for her learning needs. The good adjustment she made to it will have led to her being favourably perceived by her teacher.

Once in the secondary school Kathleen was faced with a

rather different situation. Though it was argued in chapter 6 that, in this study, the senior primary classes were not unlike the first-year secondary classes in organization and teaching methods, Kathleen happened to come from the most 'progressive' classroom to relatively more formally managed classes. The following extracts from the field notes will indicate how she adjusted to some of her secondary school classes.

Mr D 8 Some noise from the class who are bewildered by this 'triangular number sequence'. Kathleen says, 'I can't do it. I wasn't here yesterday.' Teacher gets cross. 'Look, if you can't do it I can. Do me the favour of listening. Who cares if you weren't here yesterday, we started afresh today.'

Mrs C 4 Teacher asking questions about the poem they have just heard. Kathleen whispering to Emily. She answers one question without much enthusiasm.

Mrs A 5 Tremendous noise in here today. Ian and Kathleen are throwing kisses to each other. – Kathleen is teasing the teacher. She sings the 'do re me' scale (not very accurately) whenever Mrs A turns to write on the board. Mrs A tries to ignore it. – Helen H is told to stand up. More noise. Eileen stood up also. Kathleen says, 'Please, Miss, it was the three of us to be truthful.' 'Never mind. I don't want any advice from you, Kathleen.' – More noise. Kathleen has started singing her tune again this time stamping her feet in time. – Mrs A finally catches Kathleen banging her feet. She hasn't really been trying to hide it just now.

Mrs F 3 Kathleen and Bruce are having an argument. 'You'll get smashed.' 'And you.' 'You're so heavy you'd never get up again.' They continue abusing each other while teacher writes on the board. She doesn't seem to be interested in finding out where the noise is coming from. Most of the class are writing down sentences on the board. Kathleen and Bruce still arguing and pulling faces at each other.

These four short incidents enable us to see that Kathleen's behaviour has altered considerably. In the classes of the two teachers whose control of the class was uncertain, Mrs A and

Mrs F, Kathleen became one of the most troublesome pupils. Inspection of the data on the six children perceived much less favourably by their secondary teachers than by their primary teachers reveals no common factors. Kathleen and two others come from school A(i) but this is probably not important, though it is just possible that these children (all girls) found the transition from primary to secondary school more painful than most.

The debate about teaching methods and curriculum reform tends to be carried on in terms of the superiority of one type to another. For example, is i.t.a. a better way of teaching reading than t.o.? Do pupils learn more successfully under 'progressive' conditions or is the 'traditional' approach better? In fact, these arguments are sterile. It is almost certain that for some children i.t.a. will be the better method. For others t.o. will be more satisfactory. 'Progressive' methods will suit some children. Other children will be happier with more formal techniques. The crux of the matter is to identify those children best suited to each particular approach. Compatibility grouping, as this is called, has been researched in the USA notably by Thelen (1967). However, the procedure has been to allow teachers to select for their classes those they most like teaching. So far there has been no way of predicting in advance which children are most suited to which teachers. Nor has it proved possible to match children to the classroom climate they find most satisfactory. This seems an interesting and worthwhile research problem.

But the real finding of this work is not that children differ in their ability to learn in different types of classrooms, but that most of them manage the transfer with so little difficulty. The extent of the agreement between teachers in the two sorts of schools about their perceptions of individual children has already been mentioned. In general children were perceived in the same way, either favourably or unfavourably, by teachers in primary and secondary school. The extent of the agreement was most noticeable in the formation at the end of the pupils' first term in the secondary school of a remedial class. The composition of this class is shown in Table 9.

It is only to be expected that the average IQ of these children will be very low. Again it is not surprising that they came bottom of the class in their primary school, nor that they want to leave school as early as possible. The social class average is below the average for the whole sample. But, most interesting, from the average construct ranks given these pupils by their primary teachers we can see that they are a very unfavourably perceived group. It is clear that teachers will regard these children as being of low ability, but it is less obvious that they should see them in such wholly unfavourable terms. But this is the case. The children who made up the remedial class were perceived by their primary teachers not only as *dull* and *less capable*, but also as *troublesome* and *badly behaved*. They are also generally seen as *passive, stolid, immature,* and *lacking in confidence.* Some teachers also admit to finding them *less interesting.* There

Table 9 *Data for a remedial class of 12–13-year-olds*

	N	IQ (average)	Social class (see Appendix C) (modal)	Position in primary (average)	Construct rank in primary (average)	Leaving age (modal)
Boys	8	81	7	30	28	16
Girls	7	79	7	31	28	16
Total	15	80	7	31	28	16

is no self-evident reason why teachers should perceive the poorly achieving children in their classes so unfavourably. And, in fact, they do not invariably do so. However, those children who are placed in the remedial class are not only seen as being of low ability but are also negatively perceived in all other respects. In other words, the criteria for inclusion in the remedial class is not only low ability but a completely unfavourable image in the eyes of the teacher.

It was possible to check this hypothesis. The data given in Table 9 above show the average primary class positions and IQs for these fifteen children to be 31 and 80 respectively. Among the total sample of 177 children who were transferred from the five primary schools it was possible to pick out another sample of fifteen pupils with exactly the same average IQs and nearly the same class positions. The full data are presented in Table 10.

The difference between the two groups is clear. The primary

class positions of the matched group are slightly better but this seems unimportant. The most striking difference is in the much higher construct ranks of the matched sample. This is particularly true for the girls. The message is clear. Inclusion in the remedial class is as much determined by the teacher's unfavourable perceptions of a pupil as by the pupil's ability. The reasons for this are unclear. It may be that teachers are not always aware that the low ability pupils in their classes are really poor unless they are also perceived unfavourably in other respects. Again it may be that when teachers are nominating pupils for the remedial class they prefer to lose the low ability children they favour least. Whatever the reasons are the remedial class ends up with a great many children whom the

Table 10　*Data for a sample of 12–13-year-olds matched for IQ with a remedial class*

	N	IQ (average)	Social class (modal)	Position in primary (average)	Construct rank in primary (average)	Leaving age (modal)
Boys	8	79	7	29	20	16
Girls	7	81	6	23	11	16
Total	15	80	7	26	16	16

teachers perceive very unfavourably indeed. It is important to realize that this particular function of the procedure for allocating children to the remedial class is hidden. The teachers collectively responsible for it are almost certainly unaware that this is what they are doing.

It has been noted that nearly half of the children in the remedial class came from school C. Inspection of the data reveals no common factors and it can only be supposed that the result is a matter of chance. If it is a coincidence it is one that gives some meaning to the following extract from field notes made in school C. The teacher of this class was very mobile and while the children were working at their textbooks she would continually walk around the class checking work and giving help where it was needed. All the children whose names appear in italics were placed in the secondary school's remedial class at the end of their first term in the school.

School C   The class are writing exercises in their English jotters. 'Have you forgotten, *Douglas*? Have you forgotten, *John*?' Teacher looks at the two boys who are looking blank. *John* answers, 'No, Miss, just thinking.' A boy enters the room with a pile of books. Teacher asks, 'Have you counted them?' *Andrew* calls out the number of books the boy is carrying. 'Mind your own business, *Andrew*,' the teacher tells him. She instructs the boy who has brought the books to thank Mrs Y who has sent them. Teacher looks around the class. Everyone is working. 'Sit in your chair properly, Jean,' she says. Starts to walk around the class again. Teacher at the front now. 'Are you stuck?' This is to *Peter*. 'Do you need scrap paper, *Douglas*?' 'Yes, Miss.' 'Well, do it in your jotter anyway.' – *Andrew* asks a question. Teacher goes over to him. 'Read the instruction. It tells you clearly, doesn't it?' *Andrew* obviously doesn't find it clear at all. Teacher gives up trying to explain, 'Well, try it on scrap then do it in your jotter,' she says. – Teacher walking around again. Jackie and Derek are praised, 'That's good. That's better.' She turns to *Douglas*. His work has a horizontal line which should be vertical. (Teacher is looking at arithmetic books even though children are now working at English.) Teacher explains this to him. *Douglas* looks bewildered and bored. – Teacher goes to *Douglas* again. The teacher sounds cross, 'Never mind that. Look, do that!' – Teacher back with *Douglas* again. He has stopped working. 'What's the matter with you?' she asks. *Douglas* starts to write again very unenthusiastically. Teacher notices *John*, '*John*, you're only on the first one! Look see if you can work it out on your own.' 'Derek, can you hold up your book. Then anyone who is stuck can get a clue.' Derek holds up his book. *Douglas* and *Peter* look especially uninterested. Teacher shouts at them, 'You're not interested are you?' But they still don't look at Derek's book.

This record covers a period of fifteen minutes and during that time the low ability children are constantly chivvied and chastised. It is true that this teacher moved about the class more than most but she was not noticeably exceptional in the way she treated the low-ability and unfavourably perceived children. The data in the extract have become especially interesting since so many of the children from this class ended up in the secondary remedial class. Its selection is not meant to imply that it is unique. It could be duplicated many times. The material practically speaks for itself but we can draw out one or two points. Note, for example, that many of the teacher's comments are unlikely to help the children learn. Peter and Douglas are asked if they are stuck and if they need scrap paper, but this is purely symbolic; it is clear that the teacher really means, 'Get on' or 'Hurry up' or some such exhortation. When Douglas says he would like some scrap paper he is simply told to do it in his book anyway. Andrew asks a question and just gets the book's instructions read out to him. When he still doesn't understand the teacher quite unhelpfully tells him to do it on scrap first. The problem is that he can't do it at all. Douglas is taken up about his maths immediately after the two children sitting either side of him have been praised. Finally, after unhelpful exhortations to Douglas and John the teacher tries to interest them in Derek's work. This is so crass that it may seem beyond belief, but it really did happen.

The fact is that children who have the bad luck to be un-favourably perceived by their teachers have a tough time in the classroom. It is very sobering indeed to reflect on the fact that it is not at all unusual for a primary teacher to take her class for as long as three years. It is a poor imagination that cannot foresee the almost inevitable consequences of being treated as we saw Douglas, Peter, and Andrew treated every day for three years. Educational psychology has totally (one may suspect wilfully) neglected this problem. It is true that the processes are difficult to observe, and I will not claim that I have done anything more here than attempt to bring them back into the centre of legitimate investigation, but they cannot be ignored. It is no use saying that children from low social class backgrounds do poorly at school because they are from poor backgrounds until it is known that teachers behave to them in the same way that they behave to children from higher social backgrounds. This is an assumption that is always made and never tested. It is an assumption which there is less and less reason to accept.

Chapter 9   Academic self-perception

In chapter 2 I described a procedure for testing children's knowledge of the relative abilities in their class and of their own position within it. It was found that children as young as eight years were able to make assessments of their class positions which correlated highly with those of their teacher. It has been suggested that the academic self-concept which this procedure tests is an important variable affecting educational progress. The concept ultimately derives, as I argued in chapter 5, from the symbolic interactionist theory of George Herbert Mead. Mead (1934) suggested that individuals construct a 'me' for each distinct social setting in which they find themselves. In each classroom, therefore, the child must construct a self-concept and a pattern of behaviour consistent with the expectations he perceives others to have for him. Through his interactions with others his conception of himself in relation to others and the conceptions others have of him are realized. Kagan (1967) states that interactions which convey praise, respect, and understanding lead to mutual liking and positive self-evaluations on the part of both actors, whereas interactions which convey criticism and rejection create self-derogatory evaluations.

Recent work by Barker-Lunn (1970) has investigated some corollaries of self-esteem. She found for most children 'doing well' at school was important and failure resulted in a depressingly poor self-image. One notable finding particularly relevant to my work was that a considerable number of lower-ability children in non-streamed schools had poor self-images and experienced shame at not being clever. In such cases it appeared that these children were constantly being compared – to their disadvantage – with other members of their class. There can be little doubt that low-ability children in non-streamed classes taught by teachers with a strictly traditional approach have very poor self-concepts indeed. This may seem self-evident but it is a comment on conventional methodology that nearly all previous work has concentrated on systems of teaching rather than on the behaviour of teachers. Brookover (1962), an American researcher who has looked at this problem, found similar results. In a massive longitudinal study of the effects of self-conception on school progress he noted that attention is seldom given to the development of propositions about how social background factors become translated into differential actions in the classroom.

It may be argued that in every school classroom there is a community of knowledge held by the teacher and the pupils regarding the relative abilities of the class members. In chapter 2 I reported that primary school children in non-streamed classes were able to estimate their ability with considerable accuracy. Although teachers never informed pupils of their positions in the class the correlation between the pupils' own estimates of their positions and an ability rank provided by their teacher was r. 0·71. This chapter presents a further study designed to test the extent of the agreed knowledge held by the pupils about themselves and each other. If there should prove to be wide agreement it follows from interactionist theory that the expectations of the teacher are but one aspect of this problem; the expectations pupils have for each other is the other.

In order to make a close study of the self-concepts of ability of some of the children in this sample the observed secondary class, 'Edzell', was interviewed. Each pupil was seen individually and presented with a set of thirty-five cards on each of which was written the name of one of the children in his class. The pupil was asked to sort the cards into three groups: (i) a group 'a bit more clever than you', (ii) a group 'about the same as you', and (iii) a group 'not so clever as you'. The names of the pupils placed in each group were noted. To establish the child's estimate of his position he was given those he had named 'about the same' as himself and asked to 'put them in the right order'. His own name is included in this group. If, for example, a child placed ten pupils in group (i), and twelve in group (iii), his estimate of his position must lie between eleventh and twenty-third. If the pupil then places himself fourth in group (ii) his position must be fourteenth. This procedure avoided giving children the rather tedious task of ranking thirty-five cards. The resulting positions were rank-ordered. Ties were permitted.

A second measure was obtained by counting the number of times each pupil was named by his classmates as 'more clever than me', subtracted from the number of times he was mentioned as 'slower than me'. For example, a child named as 'more clever than me' by twenty of his classmates and as 'slower than me' by twelve would receive a score of $+8$. These scores which ranged from -31 to $+34$ were ranked. Ties were permitted. This rank was assumed to correspond to the position each child was collectively seen to hold.

There are now two ranks: (i) derived from pupils' estimates of their own positions, and (ii) derived from pupils' estimates of each other's positions. These were found to be significantly correlated, r. 0.72. Analysis of the data shows that for thirteen of the thirty-three pupils tested (two were absent) the two ranks were within plus or minus 3 points. Another eleven pupils saw themselves as within plus or minus 6.5 points of their position as seen by others. Five children badly underestimated their position as seen by others and were not thought to be as poor as they thought themselves. Four overestimated their positions and thought themselves better than their classmates believed.

The interactionist theory discussed above predicts that children perceived unfavourably by their teachers will develop unfavourable self-concepts and that these will be reflected in the low class positions these children will believe themselves to have. Conversely it predicts that children favourably perceived will believe themselves to be highly placed in the class. This hypothesis may be tested by correlating the teachers' perceptions of their pupils (construct rank) with the rank derived from the pupils' own estimates of their positions. The correlation was r. 0.54, which is significant at the 0.05 level. From this it follows that the correlation between the teachers' perceptions and the pupils' estimates of each other's class positions will be high. It is, in fact, r. 0.69, a result which may be taken to reflect the high degree of agreement between the pupils' and the teachers' perceptions of the relative abilities in the classroom. It is not possible to partial out these correlations in any meaningful sense and they should be looked upon not as indicating direct causal relationships but as reflecting, perhaps inadequately, the broad agreement at the level of perception within the classroom.

The children who, in the face of this agreement between teachers and pupils about the relative abilities in the class, do not share their classmates' opinion of themselves, are especially interesting. One pupil who thought so much more of herself than her classmates was Hazel who placed herself ninth, compared to her classmates' collective estimate of her as twenty-eighth. Some explanation for this can be found from close observation of her behaviour.

Case 6   Hazel

Primary school: B
IQ: 93
Primary class position: 17th
Family size: 4

Born: February 1959
Father: Semi-skilled
Member of poorly perceived clique in primary and secondary school.

Hazel is one of those pupils the teachers agree in perceiving very unfavourably. Mrs C, for example, says she is *very annoying*, *very poorly behaved*, and tending to be *dull*. Mr D finds her *immature*, and tending to be *dull* and *less able*. Mrs A says she is *noisy*, a *nuisance*, and tending to be *dull*. Her primary teacher regarded her as *bright*, tending to be *conscientious*, and tending to be *helpful*. However, this is not to say that her primary teacher perceived Hazel favourably. Her construct rank was thirteenth out of eighteen girls. In comparison with the others she was seen very unfavourably.

Other children often mentioned Hazel during conversations and they all had much the same view; the following are typical:

Fay   I sit by Hazel usually.
RN   She's very noisy sometimes.
Fay   She isn't half!
RN   How do you feel about that? When she's noisy?
Fay   I get a red face sometimes. I tell her to stop it.

RN   You get on OK, you say, in Mrs A's lessons?

Emily   Yes, 'cus Hazel takes the mickey. I get a laugh.

Eliza   Mrs A doesn't give you the belt. She just shouts.
            Like at Hazel. She's bad.

Hazel was 'bad' in the sense that she could be alarmingly
disobedient. There is a sequence showing her at her worst in
one of Mrs A's lessons.

Mrs A 4   Mrs A has written a story on the board which
the class have to copy down. Jeannie and Mary are told
to behave. Hazel shouts out something. Teacher writes
names of noisy children on the board. Roderick, Hazel and
Eileen so far. None of them appear to take any notice.

    Teacher calls to Hazel who is teasing Jane. She tells her
to come out and bring her chair with her. Teacher gives
her a book to press on and tells her to do her work in the
passage. Jane and Kathleen watch her in giggles as Hazel
messes about trying to get her chair through the door, –
Hazel pops her head round the door, 'Miss, have you got
something to read out of a book?' she asks. 'Just get on
with what I've given you,' Mrs A tells her. Hazel goes out
grinning again. – Hazel again. 'Have you got a rubber?'
she asks the teacher. Class laugh. Teacher goes to Hazel
who protests that she has made a mistake. 'Well, just cross
it out,' says Mrs A, 'I don't want to hear from you until
the end of the period.' – Hazel back again. 'Please, Miss,
I've finished,' she calls loudly. Class laughing again.
Teacher stalks over to her. 'You haven't got at least five
sentences from each paragraph,' she says after examining
the book. Hazel is sent out again. Big production as she
plays at slouching out of the room.

This is by no means an isolated instance. Hazel often behaved
like that though at other times she would sit quietly, especially
if the teacher was reading a story Hazel found gripping. Her
own view of things is very illuminating. The following is a
transcript of one of the many conversations I had with Hazel:

RN   You don't get on well with Mrs A like with, say
       Mrs M, do you?'

HK No.

RN Why not?

HK I don't know.

RN Do you think it is because the teachers behave differently or because you behave differently?

HK I think it's because I behave differently.

RN Well, how do you behave differently in Mrs A's class from how you do in Mrs M's class?

HK Well, sometimes it's boring with Mrs A – in Mrs A's class because she doesn't give you writing or that – well, when you get writing, well, it's not so boring. It gives you something to do.

RN It gives you something to do?

HK Yes.

RN You were saying just now that Mrs M gives you things to do.

HK Yes, she always gives you scales, measures from the grid reference, from the maps, and at least you're *learning* something.

RN Whereas, – how are they different in themselves Mrs A and Mrs M?

HK Well, you're learning something from Mrs A but it's awful boring – the stories. It's all right for (names a story) but other books – it's so boring about stories.

RN Let's look at the maths. What's the most interesting thing about the maths you do with Mr D?

HK Well, sometimes you've got things like oblongs and triangles and he's drawing them and that and – the number system – we never had that before at our primary. Like your number system five. That's how we were thinking in the classroom.

RN I notice you're not so noisy in Mr D's class as you are in Mrs A's or Mrs F's, why is that?

HK At least you're learning something in Mr D's class. You do learn something with Mrs F and Mrs A but it's awful boring with Mrs A – Mrs F's all right.

RN I'm trying to pin down why it's so boring for you.

HK Well, in – she stops reading the story and that – and she's telling you something and you don't really want to listen and you start talking and that.

This, I think, makes it clear that Hazel's position was one of impatience and frustration with teachers she perceived as 'soft' and as being unable to make their lessons interesting. Hazel clearly considered herself justified in making a noise and getting some fun out of annoying teachers if they bored her. Her undisciplined behaviour, however, causes the children in the class to perceive her as academically backward. An interesting halo effect. My own feeling is that Hazel's assessment of herself is more accurate than her classmates'. She is certainly able to talk fluently about 'grid references' and 'number systems' without the 'or whatever they're called' gloss that many of the pupils will add when they are talking about newly learned concepts relating to school work. Her written work, when she did any, was accurate and lively. Hazel, however, was noisy and was poorly perceived by both her classmates and her teachers. It shows remarkable strength of character that she is able to maintain her own image of herself against the pressures and expectations set up for her by others.

Hazel perceived herself as more clever than her classmates thought her. The following study discusses a girl who underestimated herself. Mary placed herself twenty-fourth compared to her classmates' estimate of eleventh.

Case 7   Mary

School: E   Born: February 1959
IQ: 91   Father: Occupation not known
Primary class position: 13th   Member of poorly perceived
Family size: 9/youngest   clique at primary, isolate at
                                              secondary.

Mary is agreed to be generally favourably perceived. Mrs C and Mrs A see her as tending to be *bright*, and Mr D says she is *able*. Mrs A and Mrs C both agree that she tends to be *well behaved*. Mr D finds her *very pleasant*, and *very mature*. Mrs A also sees her as *mature*, and finds her *imaginative*. To Mrs C Mary is *attractive* and *lively*. Her primary teacher, also, thought well of her saying that she was *bright*, *alert*, and *knowledgeable*. It is not at all easy to see why Mary should have so low an opinion of herself.

According to Mary she 'gets on well' with most of her

secondary teachers including Mr D, Mrs C and Mrs A. She finds the work at secondary school easier than at primary. She says, and it is the only indication that she has any doubts about her ability, 'I like the way Mrs C reads stories. And poems. I like those. *I'm not good at them* but I like them and I like stories and that.' Perhaps there is one other clue. Mary has no very close friends in the class. On first acquaintance with her this seems hard to believe and the outcome of the sociometry puzzled me until I looked more closely. Mary says that her friends are Helen B, Helen H, and Eileen. But these girls do not, in fact, form a clique. Helen B is a very able girl who sits by Pat. Helen H and Eileen are also able girls who are close friends and members of a favourably perceived clique, but they do not regard Mary as belonging to their group.

Her behaviour in class may help us to understand. Mary is often noted answering questions and she normally worked hard but occasionally she would join in with Jeannie, Irene, and Kathleen who sometimes became troublesome. This was not behaviour that would make her acceptable to Helen H and Eileen (and even less to Helen B) who were especially conscientious. Mary did not seem at all settled about her position or able to make up her mind about whom she really wanted to be friends with. My own guess is that to some extent her classmates tended to overestimate her ability, perhaps they noticed her liveliness in answering questions and her desire to associate with Helen B and Helen H. (Though there is some evidence that she was able.) This extract from the field notes shows her taking a very active part in an English lesson:

Mrs C 2 Mary is with Emily. Teacher is asking questions about the poem. 'What were the courtiers doing?' Mary answers, 'They were bowing down on their knees.' 'What else were they doing?' 'They kissed his hand.' Mary again. 'Yes, what else did they do?' Mary still has her hand up. – Mary answers another question. 'They were so interested in the cardinal they didn't know what the jackdaw was doing.' . . . 'Where was he hiding?' the teacher asks. Mary calls out, 'In the belfry, Miss.' She answers several more questions. Only she, Alec, and Helen B are taking any real part in this lesson.

The other children certainly note this sort of behaviour and use it in gauging the relative abilities in the class. Mary, for some reason, does not. I have suggested that one reason for this poor self-assessment may be related to her inability to become accepted by the friendship clique to which she aspires, yet another reason may be the relatively poor perception of her held by her primary teacher. She was given a construct rank of sixteenth out of twenty-one girls and that is very low. It is possible that Mary has not so far adjusted to being rather better perceived by her new teachers.

This chapter began by discussing the results of previous work on academic self-perception. One of the most important findings was that low-ability children in non-streamed schools tended to have worse self-concepts than similar children in streamed classes. Barker-Lunn (1970) used the word 'depressing' to describe how poorly some of these children saw themselves. There were four or five such children in 'Edzell', the class primarily studied. These were children who saw almost everyone else in the class as being more clever than they and whose classmates thought that an accurate perception. It hardly needs to be said that their teachers also perceived them unfavourably. The following study will indicate that 'depressing' is an objective word in this context.

Case 8   Bruce

School: D   Born: November 1958
IQ: 90   One parent family
Primary class position: 33rd   Isolate at primary and second-
Family size: only child   ary school.

Bruce was not seen at all favourably by his teachers. Mrs A and Mrs C perceived him as tending to be *less bright* and tending to be *dull*. Mr D, who seemed to have a firmer opinion, saw him as *very much less able*. Bruce was seen by Mrs A as tending to be *retiring* and tending to be *stolid*. Mrs C and Mr D had a somewhat better opinion of him than this and respectively saw him as *lively* and tending to have a *strong personality*. His primary school teacher, however, had hardly a good word to say for him. According to him Bruce was tending to be *obstreperous*, of *low IQ*, *unassuming* and *passive*. He saw his own position in the class as about thirty-second out of thirty-five, and his classmates agreed almost exactly. They placed him at thirty-third.

Bruce's classroom behaviour may help to explain the low opinion of him that everyone, himself included, held.

Mr D 8   Teacher starts the lesson. 'Some of us started this yesterday.' Bruce interrupts. 'I wasn't here yesterday.' Mr D gets cross. 'That's why I said some of us, idiot! What's the matter with you? Don't you understand English?'

Mr D 11   Bruce and George fooling about and talking. – The class have to count the number of times each letter is used in a passage the teacher has given them from a French text-book. Most pupils understand that they have to make a frequency chart. Bruce looks lost. He is staring round the room. – Bruce waving his hand about. He wants some help I suppose. He chats to Matthew complaining that he can't tell what to do. Teacher comes to help him at last. Bruce gets told off for trying to take a short-cut. 'You were told not to take it. It's a mistake. Well, you've had it now. It's just a mess.' Teacher leaves Bruce who gives up.

Mrs A 5   Teacher is trying to get the class to read out their compositions. Great noise as people shout the names of those they want to hear read. Bruce puts his feet on the desk. More noise. 'Bruce,' calls the teacher. He puts down his feet very slowly. He is lounging about, arms outstretched, head back, feet wide apart. He looks as if he is asleep in front of a fire. – Bruce has decided to play with the window blind again. He puts it in his mouth and round his neck. He seems to be reining himself as if he were a horse. Teacher looks at him but takes no notice. – Bruce still quietly tying himself up with the window cord. – Matthew starts to join in this game. Teacher walks over to them. She has obviously had enough. They let go of the cord after a bit of argument. Bruce just slouches back without altering his attitude. He grins as Matthew starts to read his book and continues to rock back and forth on his chair.

Mrs B 1 Teacher is letting the boys form groups for science work. Bruce dashes up to Matthew. 'Oh, no,' says the teacher, 'Bruce, you are enough for one group.'
Mrs B 3 Class working very quietly at seatwork. 'Bruce?' calls teacher, 'get on with it. Dreaming. Stop dreaming!' Bruce looks blankly at the teacher who has turned back to her marking. He continues to revolve on his seat which is fitted with a screw so that it will turn round and round.

By now the reader should have got a fairly good picture of Bruce's classroom style. Although his teacher regarded him as generally poorly behaved his misbehaviour is quite different in character from the mischievousness of Kathleen, Alec or even Hazel. All of these children amused themselves (and most of their classmates) by teasing teachers whom they thought (i) soft, and (ii) boring. Bruce's misbehaviour was the product of inattention. We see him engrossed in lonely complicated games with the window-blind cord, in spinning on his chair, and lounging about clearly pretending to be somewhere else. All this behaviour is designed to remove him, existentially if not actually, from the classroom where he is so little valued. He behaves in just the same way no matter who the teacher is. The teachers accommodate to it as best they can. Mrs B indulged him with a rather heavy-handed humour. Mrs A normally ignored him. We see her interfere when Matthew also starts to play with the window cord because she knows that this will lead to squabbling. Mrs C tried to involve him in lessons by calling him to read and answer questions but gradually she gave up and eventually ignored him. Mrs B tended to indulge him. She lets him form a 'group' on his own (which means he can have a microscope or whatever all to himself), rather than have to stop all the arguments which will break out if he is placed with any of the other boys. One of the reasons why he had no friends was due to his insistence on being always right. He showed no signs of learning any better and would even challenge Alec who was universally admitted to be 'top of the class'. The following note provides a good example:

Mrs B 8 Teacher is at her desk. She speaks to Bruce who is spinning his stool upside down on the bench top. He is doing this ostensibly in order to flatten his Plasticine, but it is clearly a good game. Alec and William have finished and they are tossing coins. 'If you get it you can keep it,' says Alec. 'Heads,' William calls. 'Tails,' says Alec after spinning the coin and catching it in his palm. Bruce, who has been watching them, says, 'It's a double-headed coin.' Alec turns to him. 'If it was a double-headed coin he'd have kept it, wouldn't he?'

It was possible to see Bruce put himself in a position where he could be so effectively rebuffed time and again. I tried to find out from him how he felt about this. Here is an extract from one of the many conversations I had with him:

RN   You know when you filled in that questionnaire for me, what did you say you wanted to do when you left school?

BM   Nothing.

RN   Nothing? No, you didn't. I meant to ask you about that. I said last night, you know, I said, 'I'm going to screw his ears off in the morning.' What – you never put your friends down either, did you?

BM   No. I've not got any friends.

RN   Why not?

BM   Because I haven't none.

RN   Got no friends at all?

BM   No.

RN   But you must have someone to play with?

BM   No.

RN   Well, you sometimes sit by Matthew, don't you?

BM   But I never see him. He always goes away and plays with somebody else.

RN   Does he?

BM   Yes.

RN   What do you do at playtime then, for goodness sake?

BM   Just sit there against the wall.

RN   Do you?

BM   Yes.

RN   Haven't you got *any* friends?

BM   No.

RN   Don't you want any?

BM   Not really.

RN   Did you have any friends at School E?

BM   Yes, I had a lot of friends at E.

RN   You had a lot of friends at E. Well, where are they now, then?

BM   I just sort of fell out with them.

This makes it perfectly clear that Bruce is not feeling at all happy about his isolation in the class. His problems were enormous. He was unable to make friends with the boys in his class, he had 'fallen out' with his old friends, and he had to live with the knowledge that he was not liked by anyone at school – teachers or pupils. The accommodation he made to the classroom situation, which might essentially be defined as existential withdrawal, was uneasy. So far most of his teachers are prepared to indulge him but their attitude could easily change. Bruce seems completely resigned to his relative position in the class; he does not compete and shows no interest in work even when he can do it. It is as if he felt that if he withdrew from everything he therefore couldn't be expected to take his failure seriously. This may have been a device by which he strove to protect himself from the corollaries of his self-concept. The accommodations his teachers made to his withdrawal have been analysed. It needs to be stressed that these responses are only understandable as ways of making him fit into the class. They are designed to make the teacher's job easier; not to improve Bruce's chances of learning. Bruce had developed a system which eased the teacher's life provided that she left him alone. Most of them did.

In this chapter I have argued that from an interactionist standpoint the child can be understood to be actively engaged in working out through his day-to-day interactions in the classroom a pattern and style of behaviour from which he and others build up expectations for his future behaviour. That others in the classroom are engaged in a continual process of evaluation has been demonstrated by the high correlation between the perception a child has of his class position and the perception his classmates have of it. It is becoming clear that within the classroom there is a commonly agreed body of knowledge about the relative abilities of all its members. These results may be taken to support the interactionist theory that children are continually engaged in forming a concept of themselves and developing a consistent pattern of behaviour appropriate to this self-concept. There is evidence that the firmer these patterns of behaviour become the more unshakeable the models of them constructed by others will be and the more power their expectations will have in confirming the others' behaviour. And the models and expectations children have of each other may be as important in determining academic behaviour as those of the teacher.

At a later stage it may be possible to test the theory more rigorously. This research was carried out just ten to twelve weeks after the children had entered the secondary school and was designed to test changes in the self-concept after transfer from primary school. It can be argued that although the correlations between the pupils' view of their own and others' class positions seem high, towards the end of the year when the children have had more time to adjust to the secondary school, they will be yet higher. Moreover, the concordance between the teachers' perceptions of the pupils may also be expected to increase by the end of the year.

Chapter 10   Friendship cliques in primary and secondary school

The central theme of this study has been the development in children of a set of 'taken-for-granted' attitudes towards the self and its presentation in the classroom. This self-concept I suppose to be formed through the child's interaction with his teacher and his peers. The previous three chapters have concentrated almost exclusively upon the importance of the relationship between the teacher and the individual pupil. I believe that this relationship has a fundamental importance in structuring children's responses in school. In several case studies, however, I have argued that changes in a child's classroom behaviour, or in his view of himself, have been influenced by his relationships with his peers. For example, it was suggested (pp. 95–7) that Mary's interest and ability in her schoolwork deteriorated after she had been moved from primary to secondary school and that this may have been connected with her ambiguous friendship aspirations.

The link between the peer-group associations of children and their classroom behaviour is more important than the previous chapters, with their emphasis on the teacher/pupil relationship, may have suggested. To an observer it sometimes seems that teachers perceive the children in their class more often as members of groups or 'gangs' than as individuals with separate identities. For example, the best way of reminding a teacher of a pupil whom he has forgotten (teachers often have difficulty in remembering everyone in their classes) is to tell him who the child's friends are. In this penultimate chapter I want to redress some of the balance and show how important the friendship groups which children form in the classroom are in patterning their self-identity and their behaviour.

Studies of friendship among primary and secondary school children have been mainly carried out in streamed schools and have shown, essentially, that children tend to make friends with others of similar attitudes, attainments, and backgrounds to themselves. The literature on this subject is massive and I shall restrict my attention to a few of the more telling studies. One of the earliest studies of children's groups in primary schools described how boys in a class of ten-year-olds formed two stable, peacefully co-estisting cliques based, apparently, on the propinquity of their homes, religious denomination, and IQ; but not social class. Blyth (1960) did not investigate the pupils' attitudes and behaviour, not did he say which groups were preferred by the teacher; in fact, the teachers appeared to have little awareness of the existence of the groups. In a later study which compared friendship in streamed and unstreamed schools Willig (1963) found that girls in unstreamed classes tended to choose friends with a similar IQ to their own, but the tendency was less true for boys. In streamed classes the IQ range was, predictably, too narrow to allow children to form friendships with children greatly dissimilar in intelligence to themselves. Similarly, in streamed schools, the narrow social class range coupled with the social cleavage between the 'A' and the 'B' streams, meant that in these schools friendships were almost always between children of like social class. In the unstreamed classes, however, there was a slight tendency for children to group along class lines. An American study by Dietrich (1964) discovered no appreciable differences in the selection of friends in streamed and unstreamed schools. In both types of school there was a tendency for children to select friends of similar intelligence. In the most recent study by Barker-Lunn (1970) it was shown that primary school children seemed, on the whole, to choose each other as friends when they were of similar ability and social class. The data in this National Foundation for Educational Research (NFER) survey, however, were not analysed in a way which could reveal the characteristics of individual cliques. Children were defined as 'stars' or 'neglectees', and the research design was based on correlates of these measures of sociometric status. An examination of the characteristics of mutual pairs was also made and from this one interesting point emerged: the author suggested that some traditional teachers following formal methods may transmit their 'dislike' of below-average children to their pupils, who then tend to select friends in accordance with their teachers' own feelings.

Friendship in secondary schools has been much more extensively researched, but the studies led to the same sort of conclusions. Three recent studies are worth noting. The earliest by Hargreaves (1967) showed how low-stream fourth-year pupils in a secondary modern school rejected the 'academic', 'pupil' role, which the higher-stream pupils accepted, and created an autonomous, 'delinquent' peer culture of their own. Similar research by Lacey (1970) in a grammar school filled out this picture using the concepts of *differentiation* and *polarization* in an analysis of the way in which boys in a second-year streamed class began to make friends with those with similar attitudes towards school as themselves. Finally, in a study of streamed comprehensive schools Ford (1970) showed that social class was relatively insignificant as a factor influencing the friendship choices of the children in this sample, and it was suggested that class of aspiration might be more important.

The literature as a whole, and particularly that concerned with secondary schools, might be taken to suggest that it is the system and process of streaming which is responsible for the formation of friendship cliques differentiated by their strongly favourable or unfavourable attitudes to school. There is no doubt that this phenomenon is commonly found in streamed schools, but one may question whether streaming (though certainly an aggravating factor) actually creates it. Investigation of children's friendships in unstreamed schools would be one way to establish what sort of cliques children form under freer conditions. The research reported here was carried out, in part, to illuminate this question. The extent to which the teacher, both through deliberate manipulation and through the less conscious influences of her expectations for children, affects the creation and stability of friendships within her class, is another relatively unexplored area touched upon here.

It may be useful to remind the reader about the sizes of the different samples. The primary school sample was composed of 152 twelve-year-old children who made up the top five classes (i.e. less class A(ii) and twenty-seven absentees) in five non-streamed primary schools. The children were given a simple sociometric questionnaire during their last term. At Easter 1971, almost all the children were transferred to a single neighbourhood comprehensive school and, together with a few children from other schools, they were there formed into six non-streamed classes. These classes were given a sociometric questionnaire at the end of their first term. The form was completed by 157 children (i.e. less class 'Doune' and thirteen absentees). All are from an ordinary post-war housing scheme on the outskirts of this city.

The repertory grid technique used in this study was described in chapter 3. It provided an accurate, quantitative measure of individual teachers' personal constructs. From these constructs a scale was derived and each teacher rated each pupil on her own personal scale. From these ratings it was possible to arrive at a rank order of pupils and a child's position in this rank was taken to indicate the extent to which that child was perceived favourably or unfavourably by his teacher.

The sociometric questionnaire was straightforward. Each child was asked to write the names of three classroom friends – best friend, second friend, and next friend. From these data sociomatrices were constructed according to the following procedure:

(1) begin with the child receiving the highest number of friendship choices.

(2) enter this child's choices on the sociomatrix in their correct order.

(3) enter each of these three children's choices placing first any which they choose in common.

(4) continue in this way until the sociomatrix is completed.

(5) examine the sociomatrix for obvious groupings and rearrange as necessary so that reciprocated choices are placed as close to the central diagonal as possible.

(6) test the cliques within the sociomatrix against each other using the Mann–Whitney 'U' statistic to establish which of the groups are made up of children with high, and which with low construct ranks.

(7) rearrange the sociomatrix so that those cliques made up of favourably perceived children are placed towards the top, and those with less favourably perceived children are placed towards the bottom.

This procedure, which is similar to that of Harary and Ross (1957), gives a clear graphic view of the friendship cliques within a class.

The analysis of the final sociomatrices was simplified by the sex division. Almost invariably boys chose boys and girls chose girls; this enabled two sociomatrices, one for each sex, to be drawn up for each class.

In these five primary school classes there were 84 boys; 64 of these formed thirteen identifiable cliques, six defined as favourably perceived and seven as unfavourably perceived. Twenty boys were not members of a clique. Of the 93 girls, 72 formed twenty-one cliques, eleven defined as favourably perceived and ten as unfavourably perceived, leaving twenty-one as non-clique members.

To establish the relationship between members of a favourably perceived clique or an unfavourably perceived clique and social class a Kolmogorov–Smirnov test was performed, the

Table 11 *Association between social class and membership of favourably perceived and un-favourably perceived cliques in primary classes*

	χ^2	d.f.	p.	N
Boys	7·8	2	0·02	62
Girls	8·4	2	0·02	62
Total	15·8	2	0·01	124

results, given in Table 11, show that clique formation is significantly associated with social class.

Following Ford's hypothesis that social class of aspiration may be more important than class of origin, chi-square tests were worked between the children's job choices and membership of cliques. There was no evident relationship. The only clear outcome was that girls tended to have higher aspirations than boys.

It was not possible to administer to these children any form of test which would provide data about their attitudes towards school. Instead, they were asked to state at what age they wished to leave school, fifteen, sixteen, seventeen or eighteen. There is evidence that the response to this single question has more predictive power than a whole range of attitudinal variables. For example, in Himmelweit and Swift's (1969) study the most powerful contributing variable was the age at which a boy said

he wanted to leave school if he was free to choose. A Kolmogorov
–Smirnov test was performed between clique membership and
age of wanting to leave school. The results approach a reasonable level of significance where the boys are concerned. Very
few girls wished to leave at fifteen and most wanted to stay
on until they were seventeen or eighteen. This fits in with their
higher aspirations. The details are shown in Table 12.

A final Kolmogorov–Smirnov test was performed between
clique membership and IQ. At the age of seven the children
in this sample were given, as a matter of routine, a Moray
House picture test, the results of which were entered on their

Table 12 *Association between age of wanting
to leave school and membership of favourably
perceived and unfavourably perceived cliques in
primary classes*

	χ^2	d.f.	p.	N
Boys	5·2	2	0·10	77
Girls	1·9	2	0·50	75
Total	4·9	2	0·10	152

record cards. The results were surprising. Table 13 shows that
clique membership at the age of twelve was significantly
correlated with IQ scores obtained five years before.

On transfer to secondary school the children, together with
a small number from other schools outwith the district, were
formed into six classes. The classes were unstreamed and made
up of a number of children from each primary school class.
The primary school friendships were thus put under great
strain and most broke up. Sociometric data were obtained and
processed in the manner described above, again using the
construct ranks derived from the repertory grids completed
by the primary teachers. The cliques thus defined as favourably
or unfavourably perceived were analysed to test the association
between social class, IQ, and age of wanting to leave school.
The results were non-significant. That is to say, the new friendship cliques formed in the secondary school were completely
independent of their primary teachers' perceptions. A possible
explanation for this may be that the secondary teachers favoured

different children than the primary teachers, and that once in the secondary school the children re-formed cliques according to the perceptions of themselves held by their new teachers. One way to test this hypothesis was to obtain data about the perceptions of the secondary teachers.

We have seen that the six first-year classes were taught by some twenty teachers. It would have been ideal to ask each of them to complete a repertory grid for each of the classes. However, considerations of time, and a desire not to exhaust the goodwill of the teachers, determined that this part of the research was carried out on only one class. A class was chosen

Table 13 *Association between IQ at age seven and membership of favourably perceived and unfavourably perceived cliques in primary classes*

	χ^2	d.f.	p.	N
Boys	5·2	2	0·10	61
Girls	6·6	2	0·05	74
Total	11·3	2	0·01	135

at random and three teachers completed a repertory grid from which three sets of construct ranks for that class were derived. The agreement between the teachers about which children were favourably perceived was fairly high; a measure of concordance, 'W', was calculated to be significant at the 5 per cent level. It was thus thought reasonable to amalgamate the three rankings to one derived ranking. The friendship cliques within this class were then tested, one against the other, using the Mann–Whitney 'U' statistic, and re-ordered.

The fifteen boys in this class were then seen to be formed into two favourably perceived cliques, with four boys in each, and two poorly perceived cliques, one of three boys the other of two. There were two non-clique members. The twenty girls in this class formed three favourably perceived cliques, one of five girls, the others of two girls each. One girl was a non-clique member. These cliques were tested for association with social class, IQ, and age of wanting to leave school. The association with social class was not significant, though the trend was in the expected direction. However, in spite of the small size of the sample, the associations between IQ at age seven, and age of wanting to leave school (from a questionnaire given at secondary school) were significant at the 5 per cent and 1 per cent level respectively. Table 14 gives the details.

Table 14 *Association between membership of favourably and unfavourably perceived cliques in a secondary class*

	χ^2	d.f.	p.	N
Social class	1·0	1	non-sign	29
Leaving age	5·2	1	0·05	32
IQ at seven	12·8	1	0·001	27

At this point it may be worthwhile to describe in detail the pattern of friendships among the boys in their first year at secondary school. 'Edzell', the class I am considering here, contains fifteen boys who form four cliques. Each of these will be considered separately.

Clique I

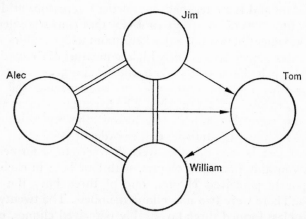

The sociogram shows reciprocated choices by double lines and unreciprocated choices by single lines, the arrow indicating the direction of choice. This represents the friendship situation three weeks after the start of the first term in secondary school.

The closest friendship was between William and Alec; they they were observed over a four-week period to sit together in 40 per cent of their lessons. These two boys were close friends at primary school E and were members there of a favourably perceived group. Tom also came from school E and though he did name William as one of his friends the choice was not reciprocated. Jim was from school A(ii) and there were no other boys from his primary school class in 'Edzell'. The average IQ of the group was 112·5 and this, though high enough, was brought down by Tom whose IQ was 91. The aspirations of the group are high. Tom and Jim wish to leave school at sixteen but both have reasonably good aspirations towards engineering apprenticeships. William and Alec wish to remain at school until they are seventeen and eighteen respectively. Their teachers perceive most of them very favourably. Their average primary school construct rank is 2·5; it is not possible to improve much on that. At secondary school they had an average construct rank of 6·7; still above the average. However, William was not nearly so well perceived by his secondary teachers as by his primary teachers and the construct rank of thirteenth given him in secondary school is reflected in the lowered average for the group. The presence of Tom and William in this group prevents one from assuming that this was a 'top' group in all respects. Alec and Jim were perceived by the class as being clever, first and eighth in the class respectively. But William was placed at fourteenth and Tom at twenty-fourth. None of the boys disagreed to any significant extent with these perceptions of their abilities.

By the middle of the second term important changes had occurred: Roderick, previously neglected, had been drawn into this group and William began to associate with clique II. These changes are interesting. Roderick was from school A(ii) where he was a member of a poorly perceived group. His construct rank was eleventh of sixteen boys, showing that he was not favourably perceived by his primary teacher. However, his construct rank at secondary school was very high; his teachers placed him second only to Alec. His IQ was 114 and his classmates estimated his position as tenth compared to his own estimate of ninth. This together with the movement of William, whose secondary teachers perceived him far less favourably than his primary teacher, illustrates well the tendency of cliques to polarize. The attitudes the clique's members held to the rest of the class should be noted.

Their attitudes to clique II were centred on George. 'He acts hard. He sort of pushes you about and that but if you argue with him and tell him where to get off . . .' (Jim). 'He's always proved wrong when you have an argument. He knocks around with all the second-year boys.' (Alec). 'And he gets B. J. [a second-year boy] to stick up for him that's why we can't touch him.' (Jim). Of clique III they commented on the relationship between Ronald and Ian. 'Oh, they're a funny pair. They're queer. They're always falling out with each other.' (Tom). 'Most of the time they're calling each other names then they're laughing at each other.' (Jim). 'Ian's got a bad temper though. He was swearing at Mrs S this morning. She got him in a really bad mood.' (Alec). As for the third boy in this clique he was written off. 'Ach, wee Ian pushed him against the wall and he went and told the headmaster.' (Tom). Bruce, the only real isolate in this class, was thought a 'big head'. 'He thinks he's a big one. In metal work the teacher says we've got to use a hacksaw. He says, "Oh, I've used a hacksaw hundreds of times". I mean we all have.' (William). 'He thinks he knows it all but he knows nothing. He's all right sometimes. It depends what mood he's in. But if he's got no pals, well he brings it on himself.' (Alec).

Clique II

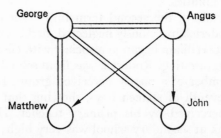

The closest friendship here was between George and Angus. They were observed over a four-week period to sit together 53 per cent of all possible occasions. George and John came from school A and Angus from school E. They were both members of unfavourably perceived groups at primary school. The average IQ of the group was 102. Their aspirations are, like those of clique I, reasonably high. Matthew wants to leave school at sixteen and become a joiner, George and Angus both wish to leave at seventeen and have thought about going to technical college. Angus has an elder brother at one of the city's universities and is aware of the possibilities that exist. This clique were just moderately perceived by their primary and their secondary teachers. At primary school their average construct rank was 7·8, and at secondary school 7. In the classroom the dynamics of the group were particularly transparent.

There are many references to the interactions between George and Angus who would wrestle with each other and throw each other's bags about whenever the class got out of hand. At these times John would try to join in but he was always rebuffed. In science these three boys, George, Angus and John, formed a work unit and it was most noticeable that George would assume control of the apparatus, microscope, burner, or whatever – and Angus and John were forced to compete between themselves to get a chance to handle the materials. In these disputes John almost always lost and could often be seen wandering about the room to see whether anyone would let him try things. Matthew didn't attempt to join these three but tended to associate with Bruce whom the teacher normally tried to keep isolated. The relationship between Bruce and Matthew was curious. Over a four-week period they were observed to sit together in 50 per cent of their lessons. However, Bruce denied having any friends and Matthew never claimed Bruce as his friend. Jim, commenting on their relationship, said, 'I don't think they're really pals. I don't know why Matthew puts up with him. He hits him all the time, you know, tapping. I think Matthew goes with him for safety more or less, because he's a wee laddie.' This is probably a fair judgment. The only close friendship in the clique is between George and Angus. John is attracted by them and, without much success, attempts to make himself noticed by them. Matthew would like to associate with them but is timid and lacks the social skills to interact with them successfully and is driven, almost it seems against his will, to go about with Bruce.

By the middle of the second term two changes had taken

place. Matthew had dropped out of his clique altogether and had consolidated his relationship with Bruce. His place had been taken by William who had developed a special acquaintance with John. This strengthened John's position in the class greatly, and George no longer found it so easy to play off John and Angus against each other.

The perceptions George and Angus had of the other friendship cliques were not favourable. Clique I they regarded as 'big heads', an epithet applied particularly to Alec. 'He thinks he's a big kid. He is quite brainy but he makes out he's the best in the class at everything.' (George). 'He's a big head. I wouldn't go around with him. He plays tig and baggy – throwing haversacks around – that's daft. Just wee ones do that.' (Angus). Of clique III they regarded the relationship between Ian and Ronald as being odd. 'Oh, they're queers. They're daft. They always tell on each other. They kick each other over their girl friends.' (Angus). Hamish they saw as being on his own. 'He sits by nobody. He's on his own again. He always gets a separate seat in case anybody sits by him.' (George). The two boys in clique IV they regarded simply as dunces. It is interesting to note their comments about Bruce. 'He shops you to all the teachers. He thinks he's better than everybody else.' (George). 'He gets on your nerves. If the teacher says do this he says, "I've done that before" and that. He gets a row for kicking his feet. He never takes PE and the teacher gets that mad at him. He's never been to the baths – never once.' (Angus). 'He tries to keep in with the teachers but they hate him, eh? All the teachers hate him. They shout at him. They pick on him. Everybody picks on him.' (George). Now joined by William there can be little doubt that this is a group of boys less than favourably perceived by their teachers. They regard themselves as 'hard' and will almost certainly develop attitudes and behaviour patterns contrary to those the school desires.

Clique III

The sociogram shows this clique to be made up of three boys. The main friendship is between Ronald and Ian who were observed to sit together over a four-week period during 38 per cent of their lessons. All three boys came from different primary schools. Ronald was from school B, Ian from school A(i), and Hamish came from a school outwith the district. At school B Ronald was a member of a favourably perceived group and his primary teacher regarded him very favourably indeed. His construct rank was first of seventeen boys. By contrast Ian was not particularly favourably perceived by his teacher at school A(i) and was given a construct rank of ninth of eighteen boys, and was a member of an unfavourably perceived group. At secondary school both boys slumped somewhat in the opinion their teachers have of them. Ronald is favourably perceived by Mrs A and Mrs C but Mr D regarded him much less favourably. Ian and Hamish are perceived by the secondary teachers to be

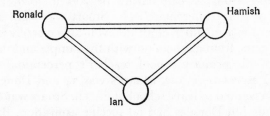

very poor. Ian's IQ score was not available, Ronald's was 84, and Hamish's 91. Ronald and Ian want to leave school at fifteen, Ronald wants to be a bus driver and Ian a joiner. Hamish has very different aspirations. He says he doesn't know what he wants to do when he leaves but expects to stay on until he is eighteen and says, 'My mum just wants me to stay on so I can go to university – take "A" levels and that.' His mother is a school teacher.

The boys are all aware that they are not a very clever lot. They all place themselves within a few points of the low positions their classmates give them. Ian, for example, places himself twenty-ninth compared to his classmates' estimates of thirty-third. In class the group were normally very quiet. Ronald hardly said a word from one week's end to the next. The same is true of Hamish. Ian was occasionally 'awkward' with teachers who crossed him, but he usually kept rather quiet. Hamish is the odd one out in this group and always tried to sit on his own in the classroom.

By the middle of the second term the friendship between

Ian and Ronald had become deeper and Hamish had dropped out leaving the other two to themselves. When I talked to all three it was evident that they did not have a shared perception of the other groups in the class. Ian and Ronald were prepared to agree that Alec and Jim were clever, but Hamish was more cautious and thought it that depended on what lessons people were in. They all, however, saw George and Angus as 'hard' and noisy.

Clique IV

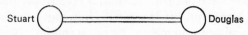

Stuart and Douglas can hardly be said to form a clique. They were from different schools. Stuart was from school B where he was a member of an unfavourably perceived group. Douglas came from a school outwith the sample and nothing is known of his primary school teacher's perceptions of him. Their IQ scores were low. Stuart's was 74 and Douglas's 79. Both boys wanted to leave school at fifteen. Stuart wanted to be a mechanic but Douglas had no specific aspiration. Both boys were perceived very unfavourably by their secondary teachers, being placed sixteenth (Douglas) and seventeenth (Stuart) out of seventeen boys. Stuart placed himself thirty in the class compared to the class's estimate of thirty-fourth. The class placed Douglas thirty-fifth, that is last of all. I did not ask Douglas to take part in the self-assessment procedure. I had some doubts that he would be able to read the names on the cards and, more importantly, I hadn't the heart to watch him place every single person in the class as 'better than me'. My reluctance shows how certain I was of the outcome. Both boys made choices to others in the class but only one was reciprocated. This was between Alec and Stuart. On Alec's part this was a purely altruistic act, he seemed to feel protective towards Stuart. It is interesting in this context to note that Douglas makes a friendship choice to Jim, also a member of clique I, and though it is not reciprocated it does indicate that there is a degree of protectiveness and help being given by the very bright boys to the very dull ones – a finding which may gladden the hearts of those of us who favour mixed-ability classes.

By the middle of the second term Stuart had been placed in the remedial stream and Douglas was left to cope as best he could on his own.

The boys in this non-streamed class provide an almost perfect example of the tendency of children to polarize into small cliques. The reality of these cliques is beyond dispute. They are revealed by the sociogram, by the statements of the children, and by the report of the teacher. Each clique usually has its own distinct attitudes towards school, its own agreed perceptions of the other cliques, and its own patterns of behaviour in and out of the classroom. Clique I is a high-ability group with high aspirations, and though they can be disruptive in lessons they are basically favourable in their attitudes to school. Clique II is a moderately favourably perceived group; two of them do tend to be disruptive but their abilities and their aspirations are both fairly high. Clique III is an unfavourably perceived group with low abilities and mostly low aspirations. Clique IV is a distinctly unfavourably perceived group of two boys of very low ability.

As far as can be seen social class is of little importance in determining the boys' choice of friends. Almost all their fathers are employed in skilled trades and little meaningful distinction can be made between them. Alec, Jim, George, and Hamish have fathers who are employed in clerical or supervisory work and it is notable that all four have higher aspirations than most of the others. However, the figures are certainly not significant in any statistical sense and they don't seem to influence their choice of friends.

These results confirm the findings of Barker-Lunn (1970), Lacey (1970), and Hargreaves (1967), that social class has at least some influence on the friendship choices of children. But other factors seem more important. The cliques can be seen to be made up, predominantly, of children either favourably or unfavourably perceived by their teachers. This is true in the primary school and in the secondary school. It is particularly interesting to note that when cliques formed in the secondary school were ordered on the sociomatrix according to the children's construct ranks given by their primary teachers, there was no significant relationship between this order and social class and IQ. Only when the construct ranks given by secondary teachers were used to re-order the cliques were the expected associations again found. In other words, once transferred to the secondary school, the perceptions of the primary school teachers did not affect the formation of friendship cliques. But the perceptions of their new secondary teachers may have done so. There seem to be four substantive conclusions to be drawn from this research: (i) whether taught in streamed or in non-streamed schools children will form cliques which will be distinguishable by their different attitudes towards school, (ii) where cliques are being formed within a population where there is a sufficient spread of IQ and social class, these factors will be reflected in the pupils' friendship choices, (iii) cliques will, from an early stage, develop distinct identities, which are important in fashioning the self-identities of individuals, but these will not, at least among Scottish twelve-year-old boys, reflect either adult subcultural differences or a national 'youth culture', (iv) the cliques within a class will be identifiable as being made up of children either clearly favourably perceived or clearly unfavourably perceived by their teachers.

For schools these findings do not seem hopeful. Next year the children in this sample will be formed into three banded streams. It is as near to a sociological certainty as anything can be that most of the boys in clique I are headed for band 1, those in clique II for band 2, and those in clique III for band 3. As for the two boys in clique IV, Stuart has already 'been placed in the remedial class. Schools will have little trouble with the clique I children who will learn almost anything they are given and will only normally become troublesome when provoked (by, for example, boredom or weak discipline), but the children in cliques II and III will tend to become increasingly difficult as they get older. It is precisely these children that the school most needs to teach (the others will learn anyway) and it is precisely these they do not teach. Paying more attention to the rise of disaffected cliques of children is only one small aspect of better teaching but it certainly does need attention.

Chapter 11   Conclusion

Each separate research in this study of learning in classrooms has contributed to a central theme. It has been assumed that the essential cultural messages of the school are conveyed through an incalculable number of interactions between teacher and pupil. These messages are only marginally concerned with school learning in the normal sense of the term but they have everything to do with the child's status, with his self-image, and with his aspirations for the future. Again and again it has been shown in these pages that teachers' perceptions of their pupils are closely correlated with the children's ability and behaviour.

Most of the hypotheses which developed during the course of the work have been confirmed. The discovery that children, even when taught in unstreamed primary classes, were well aware of their position in the class was a cornerstone of the research. Having demonstrated that children know how they are seen by their teachers it was possible to go on to investigate how this knowledge might affect their behaviour.

To a considerable extent the success of the study has been due to the power of the repertory grid technique to reveal meaningful dimensions of teacher perception which could be significantly related to children's ability and to the formation of their friendship groups. Using this technique it was possible to show that teachers normally saw their pupils not only – nor even mainly – in terms of their academic ability but much more generally in terms of their personality. The repertory grid could be a powerful instrument in the analysis of inter-personal perception in the classroom and I have suggested several ways in which teachers' constructs might be used to structure and interpret observations of pupil behaviour.

An unexpected outcome of the research was the finding that at classroom level pupils' social origins seemed of little importance. For the sample in this study social class was not correlated with measures of ability. However, and it is worth repeating, several teachers who thought social class an important determinant of ability were wrong when asked to assess the background of children in their class. These teachers believed the slower and less likeable children to come from poor homes, but objective data showed their backgrounds to be no different from those of any others in the class. It could be that the emphasis placed by sociologists on the corollaries of class origin can mislead teachers to suppose a relationship between low social class and low ability even where it does not exist.

Some hypotheses, however, have not been borne out by results. In particular I had expected there to be much greater differences between teaching practices in primary and secondary classes than in fact existed in the schools I observed. For example, as great a percentage of the curriculum was spent on written seatwork in four of the five primary classes studied as in the first-year classes of the comprehensive school to which they were transferred. Even so it was interesting to find that most of the boys seen by secondary teachers as lacking effort or being poorly behaved were not from liberally run 'progressive' primary classes (as many teachers believed) but from very strictly regimented 'traditional' classes. Less satisfying was the discovery that teaching methods in most primary school classes bore little resemblance to recommended practice. Those who work in schools are aware of the enormous gap between theory and practice. This is another area where there is a paucity of research, and yet the divorce of educational theory from classroom practice is probably more responsible for the professional cynicism of teachers than any other aspect of the job.

Perhaps because there were only minimal differences between the teaching methods of primary and secondary teachers, most children had little trouble in managing the transfer. But, of course, there were instances where a child's behaviour did change after the move. Several children, boys particularly, became more difficult to control and actually behaved quite punitively towards some inexperienced secondary school teachers. As a result, the work of these boys deteriorated and the view their teachers had of them became less favourable.

A further indication that the repertory grid is getting at a vital aspect of classroom reality became apparent when a remedial stream was formed at the end of the children's first term in secondary school. The boys and girls allocated to this class were perceived very unfavourably by their teachers. In fact, they were perceived far less favourably than a group with exactly comparable primary school class positions and IQs. There seems to be no other explanation for this than that teachers, wittingly or unwittingly, were selecting children whom they perceived particularly unfavourably for the remedial class. It goes without saying that teachers will deny favouring some children at the expense of others. But it is rather less obvious why they invariably deny having likes and dislikes about children and always claim to be scrupulously fair towards them all. It is wishful thinking of the most naïve kind to believe this. Psychiatrists and social workers have long recognized that, being human, they can sometimes have unpredictable and irrational reactions to their patients and clients. In these professions it is accepted that where there is a 'personality clash' then the case had better be transferred to another worker. As a profession teachers refuse to recognize this problem. As individuals it seems they solve it by moving the children they most dislike into the remedial classes. This is another area of teacher behaviour that has remained taboo to research workers but even though there is unlikely to be full-scale research with this proposition as its major hypothesis it is time that the idea was brought into the open.

In the end this reasearch has worked its way towards an interactionist view of the classroom. I assume that teachers' expectations do affect a child's school performance in so far as they affect the development of the child's self-image. There is evidence that a child's self-perception is strongly influenced by the teacher's perceptions of him. In the classroom there is a common agreement about the relative positions in the class of all its members. Each child knows his position with respect to that of everyone else. And taken as a whole the estimates of the class closely match ability rankings made by the teacher. In three case studies it was possible to analyse in some detail the workings of the self-concept in individual children. Perhaps the most sobering of these was the case of Bruce. This was a boy who had no friends, had despaired of his chances of doing anything worthwhile in school, and was developing an appallingly poor view of himself. But none of his teachers made any noticeable efforts to re-integrate him into the class. The teachers' main concern was to reduce his potential as a troublemaker and this they sought to do by isolating him: a treatment which must inevitably increase his alienation from the rest of the class and reinforce his negative self-image.

The analysis of friendship groups proved to be more important than social class factors. It seems that in each class there can be identified one or more cliques made up primarily of children favourably perceived by teachers and one or more cliques made up of children unfavourably perceived. Each group develops its own distinct and corporate identity which is formed from and in turn helps to fashion, the self identities of its individual members.

Several times I have suggested that social class factors may be a less important determinant of ability than is commonly believed. Of course, it is a matter of sociological commonsense that children from low social class backgrounds do poorly at school. I am not in any sense attempting to say that this is not true. However, the reasons that are commonly advanced to explain the power of this variable are more open to debate.

Because social class is a categorization applied to pupils it is almost always assumed that the reasons for the relative failure of working class children in the educational system must lie in the child. It is rarely understood that every such account implies a corollary on the part of the teacher. It is argued, for example, that working class children use language structures which prevent them understanding the language used by teachers. But this argument may be turned on its head. Teachers may be unsuccessful in teaching working class children because they are unable to accommodate their language structures to those of the children they teach. Actually, the argument makes more sense like this. After all, if language matching is what is needed then trained teachers ought to be more capable of bringing it about than young children. To take another example, teachers often argue that working class children are slower and less interested than are middle class children in learning what they have to teach. From the teacher's point of view this is undoubtedly true. But to the child it probably looks as if the teacher goes too fast and gives uninteresting lessons. The idea that the working class child is inherently less educable is all too pervasive. Those who think like this tend to hold one of two attitudes. Either they believe that nothing can be done for working class children (the right wing position) or they put their faith in pre-school programmes and compensatory education (the left-wing position). Both are wrong and for similar reasons. The working class child is reified by their determinism. All genetic and sociological factors are mediated and realized through the interaction between the teacher and the child in the classroom. If, for working class children, the outcome of these interactions is a sense of failure, then the responsibility is as much that of the teacher as of the child.

It is the context in which these interactions take place that I have attempted to study. The recent work of the empiricist psychologists into the effects of 'teacher expectations' have been the first, and very welcome, signs of a movement towards the investigation of the power of the teacher to determine the school career of her pupils. I have argued that this research is unlikely to demonstrate conclusively the effects of the phenomenon it is investigating. There are two reasons for thinking this. Theoretically the approach seems naïve. Although the central concept is from Mead's symbolic interactionism, the implications of this theory are never mentioned, let alone spelled out. Again, it seems that the reluctance of the psychologists in this field to spend time actually in classrooms may be less advantageous than they believe.

This tendency to shy away from the actuality of the classroom is rather curious. People who study animals are moving in just the opposite direction: towards reality. Until recently the scientific study of animal behaviour (as opposed to studies by naturalists which are regarded as anecdotal) was conducted by zoologists in zoos, and 'psychologists' in laboratories. During the last twenty years other scientists have begun to observe in a controlled and systematic way the behaviour of animals in their natural habitat. Their success has been impressive. It is now clear that the behaviour of animals (lions and the great apes, for example) in the wild, is very different from their behaviour in cages. In particular, the full range of a species' social behaviour and its complex interaction with its environment, can only be explored using the concepts and methods of the ecologists.

Odd as it seems, the study of human behaviour is still in very much the same state as was animal behaviour before the ecologists. Practically all the information we have to offer to, for example, student teachers about child behaviour is derived from either clinical observation of children with disturbances of one sort or another, or from studies of normal children in the abnormal setting of the psychologist's laboratory. Almost all we know about the behaviour of normal children in the classroom (which is what the teacher wants to know about) is based on the reports of teachers. And teachers are not particularly good sources of unbiased observation, if only because it is impossible to do two jobs – teach and observe – at the same time. In this work it has been my intention to help bring the study of classroom processes into the centre of educational sciences and to promote participant observation as a legitimate method of enquiry.

In any study of human ecology it is important to take into account the attitudes of individuals to each other. In animal studies we cannot do this because there is no possible way of examining the attitudes of animals. With human beings we can, and if we are not to be absurdly reductionist, we must.

Jackson's (1969) analysis of the conditions of learning in the classroom is the only serious attempt to formulate a conceptual schema for the understanding of classrooms. Jackson saw three central messages which the classroom as a place for teaching and learning in, must necessarily transmit. The child must learn (a) to live in a crowd, (b) under constant evaluation, and (c) under conditions of power. The main task of the infant teacher is to provide an environment in which small children can learn how to interact with each other in a way acceptable to adults. By the time children reach the junior school this lesson has been well learned. One of the ways in which children do adjust to the problem of living, day after day, with a crowd of others is to select out of that crowd a small number of significant others with whom to interact for recognition and support.

In the last chapter some of the details of this 'selecting out' were examined. In the classroom, because of the emphasis on scholastic achievement, children do tend to make friends with each other when they perceive their alikeness in this respect. Some of the ways in which children perceive this likeness have been detailed in chapters 2 and 9. The really fascinating thread of evidence is that relating to the formation of friendship cliques in the secondary school. When pupils moved from the primary school, where the friendship cliques were seen to be made up of children either favourably or unfavourably perceived by their teachers, the primary school friendship cliques broke up and the pupils formed new friendships. It was seen that these new cliques were not made up of children who had been favourably or unfavourably perceived by their primary school teachers. However, and it is this I find most significant, when the perceptions of the secondary school teachers were obtained, the new friendship cliques reflected the perceptions of the new teachers fairly exactly. There are two possible interpretations which may be placed on this finding. It may be that teachers' perceptions of pupils are influenced by the company those pupils keep (which seems very likely), or it may be that when children make friends they are influenced by the perceptions their teachers have of them. It is probably a mistake to see these processes as distinct to the extent that they can be independently measured. The distinction seems logical but the dynamic interrelationship between them probably makes it impossible to determine the question by research.

It is important to understand this dynamic. It is very easy for the researcher to fall into the trap of thinking in terms of this factor or that factor, in terms of 20 per cent of the variance to this determinant and 10 per cent to that. The argument between the hereditarians and the environmentalists has been fought out in this narrow rut for decades with little understanding that the really important question to ask is how the individual works out for himself the effects of the two determinants on his life.

I have tried to demonstrate that the constant evaluation Jackson says children must learn to cope with in the classroom comes not only from the teacher but from each other. The effect this has on the self-concepts of the pupils and the patterns of behaviour they adopt in the classroom have been problems I have attempted to study. The most important point to understand about this evaluation is that it is not wholly (nor even mainly) about academic matters. The personal constructs teachers use in the evaluation of their pupils have been established in this study to be centred around the pupils' behaviour. Teachers are concerned about their pupils' liveliness, sociability, and simply how likeable they are.

In at least two respects this research has shown a relationship between the evaluations children make of themselves and of each other, and the type of classroom organization. The first is from chapter 2 where it was shown that junior school children in three non-streamed classes had a good knowledge of their relative abilities in the classroom. A close examination of these results suggests that it was the children in the class 'streamed by table' who were more aware of their relative abilities than children from classes where mixed grouping was practised. The data presented in chapter 6 showing that children from tightly organized, rigorously controlled primary school classrooms were rated by their secondary teachers as lacking effort and being poorly behaved, provides a second thread of evidence for the argument that the organization of the classroom has an important influence on the pupils' behaviour. It is extremely interesting to find a relationship between the rule-boundness of a school system and the perceptions held by the teachers of their pupils.

The research reported here has in another way looked at the differences between school systems. Bernstein (1971) has carefully analysed the nature of the transmission of learning in schools in terms of three message systems. *Curriculum*, which defines what is valid knowledge, *pedagogy*, which defines what is valid transmission, and *evaluation*, which defines what is a valid realization of knowledge. This is an elegant set of concepts. Curriculum is said by Bernstein to exist in two ideal types: one is the collection type which may be based on either a course of study or on a specialized subject, and the other is the integrated type which may be either teacher based or teachers based. In chapter 6 I described how the primary school curriculum actually tended to resemble the collection type whereas the secondary school, again contrary to expectations, seemed to be moving towards an integrated type.

Bernstein, arguing theoretically, has suggested that the change from an integrated relationship, where the connections between branches of learning are emphasized, to one of collection, where the contents stand in a closed relationship to each other, may have profound importance for the assumptions children make about the nature of learning, and what is valid learning or not. The child at school is socialized into the acceptance of certain modes of thinking about learning. He learns very early what is pedagogical knowledge and what is not. He learns what is the commonsense knowledge of his classmates and what is the uncommonsense knowledge of the school. Bernstein calls this boundary (which may be of varying strength) between what may be brought into the pedagogical relationship and what may not, the pedagogical frame. It is argued that children are socialized into frames which discourage connections with everyday activities.

The change from primary to secondary school ought, one might think, to bring about a fundamental change in the nature of the children's thinking about knowledge. In fact, the real change occurs within the primary school. As the child moves from the infants to the juniors and from there to the senior class he is exposed more and more to the differentiation between learning and non-learning. The very small child in the infant school does have an integrated day. He does work in small groups. And at this stage his teacher does not organize and encourage competition between himself and his classmates. In the infant class activities have not yet become subjects, though *play* with sand, water and Plasticine does soon become differentiated from *work*, like writing and reading. The former are joint activities carried out rather noisily, the latter are done individually and in near silence. The former become play and the latter work. This message is continually reinforced as the children go through the school. It is a message that is fully learned by the time the child moves to secondary school.

One of the insights of social observers has been the realization that the staff of any institution evolve what may be thought of as a theory of human nature. School teachers' perceptions of their pupils obviously relate to some such intuitive theory about the nature of the pupil. Each teacher has her own idea of what the ideal pupil should be. Goffman (1961) has argued that the inmate of a mental hospital can adopt one of several attitudes. He can take the 'intransigent line' and rebel, he can become 'colonized' and lead a stable and contented existence, he can become 'converted' and act out the role of ideal patient, he can 'play it cool' which offers the maximum chance of getting out physically and psychologically undamaged, or he can take the line of 'situational withdrawal' and opt out of any significant interaction with the environment. This is a very useful way of looking at the sorts of adjustments which children make to school. Most of the children do 'play it cool', that is they keep out of trouble, and while not volunteering for activities or taking a major part in things they give the impression of having just enough involvement to avoid being seen as intransigent. The 'intransigent' line is, as many teachers know to their cost, a fairly common one. The pupils who take this line are non-co-operative, deliberately awkward, insolent, and ever alert for signs of weakness on the part of the teacher. These intransigent pupils are nearly always able to set the tone for the class. The reason for this is pretty simple. The children all have certain definite and precise expectations of how teachers should behave. First among these is that the teacher should keep order. If she manifestly cannot keep order most pupils regard the teacher as having broken the rules and therefore consider the intransigent children as justified in teasing her.

During all the time I have been engaged in this reasearch I have had to express my opinions about education – or more prosaically and accurately 'what goes on in schools' – in rather guarded terms. But now that everything is finished I think it would be wrong to conclude without saying what I think might be done to improve the quality of our children's lives in school. It is difficult to be optimistic but my research, which argues that the teacher has a significant influence on her pupils, is at least more hopeful than the gloomy determinism which prevails in research circles at the moment.

For example, Donnison's (1972) study sponsored by the NFER and only the latest of a long series of similar reports, has effectively concluded that no change in the school is going to make any difference to the underachievement of children from poor backgrounds and that only a complete change in the attitudes of parents will have any effect. If this is true; if the schools can only reinforce existing class differentials in ability, if teachers are unable to find suitable approaches for working class children, if educational researchers are forced to say that only changes in the attitudes of the children's parents will make any difference; then that is real pessimism. But I do not believe this tale.

Occasionally, one sees a class where every child is working at full pitch; right up to the limit of his potential. A visit to a class like this is a moving experience. For a long time afterwards one finds the ordinary standard unbearable. But to a great extent the 'ordinary standard' is a result of the almost complete lack of support the ordinary class teacher gets from everyone around him. It is fair to say that most newly qualified teachers are keen to try out the methods they have learned. Some are lucky. They find schools where their enthusiasm is valued and where all the staff have compatible views about what they should be doing. Others, perhaps still a majority, are less fortunate. They end up in schools where the College's ideas about team teaching, group methods and integrated studies are unwelcomed, where they are given little personal encouragement, and where half the staff have fallen into the demoralized cynicism that is the occupational disease of the teaching profession. For the novice teacher this experience can be traumatic. He is at once de-skilled and left to get on in the old way as best he can. In most schools like this nothing is too obviously wrong. Everything goes smoothly enough and there is little trouble. There is an established daily routine and such a sense of taken-for-grantedness settles over the school that no other way of running it seems possible. But there are other ways and if the local authorities were determined enough these schools could be transformed.

I am already uneasy at suggesting that teachers should do this and should not do that. Exhortations are generally an ineffective way of changing things. But what is needed, I think, is a great effort to raise the level of consciousness of the ordinary teacher. This means more teacher centres, more in-service training courses, more advisers in schools, more real support for young teachers, more materials, more auxiliaries and, above all, a recognition that new approaches must be encouraged and financed. The three years I have spent as an observer in schools have not made me in any way anti-teacher (though I have met a few whom I would recommend for urgent re-training in a

profession where they do not come into contact with children);
rather they have made me deeply aware of the ordinary teacher's
plight. Many of the teacher's carefully preserved professional
rights are more or less worthless. For example, in theory the
teacher is in sole charge of his own classroom, but in practice
he dare not introduce significant changes unless most other
teachers follow him. No teacher can afford to act differently
from the rest of the staff. If the school is intensely competitive
and the children are commonly given exams and tests, any
new teacher must do the same; the children and the other
teachers will let him know that this is expected of him. Similarly,
if the school is one in which corporal punishment is the customary way of dealing with misbehaviour any teacher who tries to
stand against it will find life difficult. Major changes in approach
must be supported by the local authority as a matter of policy.
We know that efforts to change the atmosphere and practices
in a large number of schools through the determined efforts of
the local authority can be done. Leicestershire County and
the West Riding of Yorkshire are well-known examples. The
other 120 educational authorities in England and Wales are
somewhat less well known for their efforts. If it is more hopeless
to urge them to act than to wish that the attitudes of working
class parents would miraculously change, then things are really
bad.

Appendix A

A scale for measuring institutional control in schools

Section I: The school outside the classroom.
  1 Are playgrounds segregated by sex?
  2 Are corridors supervised at break and other times when pupils enter or leave school?
  3 Are pupils required to line-up on entering school?
  4 Are there any school punishments, e.g. lines or detention?
  5 Is there a set of coded school rules?
  6 Are pupils required to wear uniform?

Questions 1, 2 and 3 deal with the direct supervision of the children about the school premises and grounds; questions 4 and 5 deal with the enforcement of these rules; and question 6 provides a measure of pupils' autonomy which the school may or may not grant.

Section II: The school classroom.
  7 Are children provided access to classroom outside lesson time?
  8 Are there class monitors?
  9 Is seating arranged in groups or rows?
  10 What degree of movement does the teacher permit?
  11 Is seating self-ordered?
  12 Are pupils awarded points or stars or arranged in teams?

Questions 7, 8 and 12 look at the rules the teacher makes and the way they are enforced; questions 9, 10 and 11 measure the degree of personal autonomy they are permitted.

This is an *ad hoc* scale drawn up after considerable experience of the aspects of primary schools it was designed to measure; that is, the extent and power of the school to limit and restrict the behaviour of its pupils. Items which do not discriminate have been discarded at the planning stage and only those which do have been retained.

Appendix B

The personal construct systems of three secondary teachers

Mrs A

1 Willing to work	unwilling to work
2 Sensible	silly
3 Well behaved	nuisance
4 Quiet	noisy
5 Bright	less bright
6 Mature	immature
7 Outgoing	retiring
8 Imaginative	stolid

Mrs C

1 Friendly	annoying
2 Well behaved	less well behaved
3 Bright	dull
4 Lively	lumpish
5 Memorable	unmemorable
6 Attractive	less attractive
7 Small	large
8 Sociable	less sociable

Mr D

1 Gregarious	less sociable
2 Pleasant	less likeable
3 Outgoing	shy
4 Mature	immature
5 Independent	easily led
6 Able	less able
7 Strong 'personality'	weaker 'personality'
8 Consistent	inconsistent

Appendix C

Social class and IQ measurement

Social class was measured on an eight-point scale. The scale, with the number of pupils falling into each group, is given below.

1	Professional	3
2	Lower professional	3
3	Clerical	28
4	Supervisory/Manual	33
5	Self-employed	7
6	Skilled manual	53
7	Semi-skilled manual	28
8	Unskilled manual	28

Of the remaining twenty pupils six were from one-parent families, and for fourteen no data were available.

A Moray House Verbal Intelligence Test was administered to the children in this sample at the age of seven. The average IQ was 91·6. The breakdown of the distribution given below may be useful.

−74	12
75–84	22
85–94	46
95–104	52
105–114	31
115–124	17
+125	2

The sample described here is the secondary school sample. See pages 43–4.

References

ANDERSON, K. (1961) *The Harrap Spelling Books (iv)*, Harrap.

BANNISTER, D. and MAIR, J. M. M. (1968) *The Evaluation of Personal Constructs*, Academic Press.

BARKER-LUNN, J. C. (1970) *Streaming in the Primary School*, NFER.

BARNES, D., BRITTON, J. and ROSEN, H. (1969) *Language, the Learner and the School*, Penguin.

BECKER, H. S. (1970) *Sociological Work*, Allen Lane.

BERG, L. (1969) *Risinghill: Death of a Comprehensive School*, Penguin.

BERNSTEIN, B. (1971) 'On the classification and framing of educational knowledge' in M. F. D. Young (ed.), *Knowledge and Control*, Collier Macmillan.

BLISHEN, E. (1969) *The School that I'd Like*, Penguin.

BLYTH, W. A. L. (1960) 'The sociometric study of children's groups in English schools', *British Journal of Educational Studies*, vol. 8, no. 2, pp. 127–47.

BROOKOVER, W. B. and PATTERSON, A. (1962) *Self-concept of Ability and School Achievement*, Michigan State University Press.

BROWN, R. (1965) *Social Psychology*, Free Press.

BURSTALL, C. (1970) 'French in the primary school: some early findings', *Journal of Curriculum Studies*, vol. 2, no. 1, pp. 48–58.

CAVE, R. (1968) *All Their Future*, Penguin.

CENTRAL ADVISORY COUNCIL FOR EDUCATION (1954) *Early Leaving* (Gurney-Dixon Report), HMSO.

CENTRAL ADVISORY COUNCIL FOR EDUCATION (1960) *Fifteen to Eighteen* (Crowther Report), HMSO.

CENTRAL ADVISORY COUNCIL FOR EDUCATION (1967) *Children and their Primary Schools* (Plowden Report), HMSO.

DIETRICH, F. R. (1964) 'Comparison of sociometric patterns of sixth grade pupils in two school systems: ability grouping compared with heterogeneous grouping', *Journal of Educational Research*, vol. 57, pp. 507–12.

DONNISON, D. (1972) *A Pattern of Disadvantage*, NFER.

DOUGLAS, J. W. B. (1964) *The Home and the School*, MacGibbon & Kee.

DOUGLAS, J. W. B., ROSS, J. M. and SIMPSON, H. R. (1968) *All our Future*, Peter Davies.

DOWNIE, N. M. and HEATH, R. W. (1970) *Basic Statistical Methods*, Harper.

ESLAND, G. M. (1971) 'Teaching and learning as the organization of knowledge' in M. F. D. Young (ed.), *Knowledge and Control*, Collier Macmillan.

FLANDERS, N. A. (1970) *Analysing Teaching Behaviour*, Addison-Wesley.

FLOUD, J. E. and HALSEY, A. H. (1957) 'Intelligence tests, social class, and selection for secondary schools', *British Journal of Sociology*, vol. 8, no. 1, pp. 33–9.

FLOUD, J. E., HALSEY, A. H. and MARTIN, F. M. (1957) *Social Class and Educational Opportunity*, Heinemann.

FORD, J. (1970) *Social Class and the Comprehensive School*, Routledge & Kegan Paul.

FRASER, E. (1959) *Home Environment and the School*, University of London Press.

GARFINKEL, H. (1969) *Studies in Ethnomethodology*, Prentice-Hall.

GOFFMAN, E. (1961) *Asylums*, Doubleday.

GOODACRE, E. J. (1968) *Teachers and their Pupils' Home Background*, NFER.

HARARY, F. and ROSS, I. C. (1957) 'A procedure for clique detection using the group matrix', *Sociometry*, vol. 20, pp. 205–15.

HARGREAVES, D. H. (1967) *Social Relations in a Secondary School*, Routledge & Kegan Paul.

HENRY, J. (1963) *Culture Against Man*, Random House.

HIMMELWEIT, H. T. and SWIFT, B. (1969) 'A model for the understanding of school as a socializing agent' in P. H. Massen *et al.* (eds.), *Trends and Issues in Developmental Psychology*, vol. 2, Holt, Rinehart & Winston.

HOLT, J. (1966) *How Children Fail*, Pitman.

HOLT, J. (1970) *The Underachieving School*, Pitman.

HUDSON, L. (1966) *Contrary Imaginations: a Psychological Study of the English Schoolboy*, Methuen.

HUDSON, L. (1972) *The Cult of the Fact*, Cape.

JACKSON, B. (1964) *Streaming: an educational system in miniature*, Routledge & Kegan Paul.

JACKSON, B. and MARSDEN, D. (1962) *Education and the Working Class*, Routledge & Kegan Paul.

JACKSON, P. W. (1969) *Life in Classrooms*, Holt, Rinehart & Winston.

KAGAN, J. (1967) 'On the need for relativism', in L. Hudson, *The Ecology of Human Intelligence*, Penguin, pp. 134–56.

KELLY, G. A. (1955) *The Psychology of Personal Constructs*, Norton.

KITTO-JONES, A. (1958) *Spotlight on English*, Gibbon.

KLEIN, J. (1965) *Samples from English Cultures*, Routledge & Kegan Paul.

KOUNIN, J. (1970) *Classroom Discipline and Management*, Holt, Rinehart & Winston.

LACEY, C. (1970) *Hightown Grammar: the school as a social system*, Manchester University Press.

LAMBERT, R., BULLOCK, R. and MILLHAM, S. (1970) *A Manual to the Sociology of the School*, Weidenfeld & Nicolson.

LAWTON, D. (1968) *Social Class, Language and Education*, Routledge & Kegan Paul.

MCCALL, G. J. and SIMMONS, J. L. (eds). (1969) *Issues in Participant Observation*, Addison Wesley.

MAYS, J. B. (1965) *Education and the Urban Child*, Liverpool University Press.

MEAD, G. H. (1934) *Mind, Self and Society* (ed. C. W. Morris), University of Chicago Press.

NEILL, A. S. (1968) *Summerhill*, Penguin.

NISBET, J. and ENTWHISTLE, N. J. (1969) *The Transition to Secondary Education*, University of London Press.

PARTRIDGE, J. (1968) *Life in a Secondary Modern School*, Penguin.

PEDLEY, R. (1969) *The Comprehensive School*, Penguin.

PIDGEON, D. A. (1970) *Expectation and Pupil Performance*, NFER

ROSENTHAL, R. and JACOBSON, J. (1968) *Pygmalion in the Classroo m*, Holt, Rinehart & Winston.

SNOW, R. (1969) 'Review of "Pygmalion in the Classroom" by Rosenthal and Jacobson', *Contemporary Psychology*, vol. 14, pp. 197–9.

THELEN, H. A. (1967) *Classroom Grouping for Teachability*, Wiley.

THORNDIKE, R. L. (1968) 'Review of "Pygmalion in the Classroom" by Rosenthal and Jacobson', *AERA Journal*, vol. 5, no. 4, pp. 708–11.

WATSON, T. F. (1954) *Holmes' New Comprehensive Arithmetic (iv)* Holmes & McDougall.

WILLIG, G. J. (1963) 'Social implications of streaming in the junior school', *Educational Research*, vol. 5, no. 2, pp. 151–4.

WISEMAN, S. (ed.) (1964) *Education and Environment*, Manchester University Press.

Index